The Bubbe Meise and Other Stories

Bubbe Meise: A grandmother's fable. An "old wives tale." An untrue story. Sometimes related to superstition. Often, an Aaron Zevy short story.

D1518431

The Bubbe Meise and Other Stories

Aaron Zevy

TUMBLEWEED PRESS, INC.

The Bubbe Meise and Other Stories

Aaron Zevy

Edited by Jules Lewis
Copy edit by Heather Karbi and Marianne Last
Cover design by Tatiana Sayig, Photo by Ryan McVay on Getty Images
Book design and story covers by Helen Prancic
Photographs courtesy of the Zevy Family
Stock Photos: 123rf.com, Alamy, artistshot.com, Darren Tunnicliff, Lakewood Fogels, pixabay.com, stocksy.com, Todd Rosenberg Photography, Unsplash.com and Wikimedia Commons
Song lyrics: Sinner's Prayer, Slaid Cleaves and Rod Picott

ISBN: 9798675126095

CONTENTS

THE RUMOUR

Photograph © Darren Tunnicliff

I have since cut down a lot but there was a time when I used to have quite a lot of sugar with my coffee. This prompted friends, family, and the occasional waiter to make a joke which I heard so often that I would often be surprised if it was not made at all.

"Why don't you have some coffee with your sugar." Which is funny enough and I laughed the first hundred times I heard it.

This story is from back before I cut down. I think it might have been in 1990. I was having a cafe latte, the Israelis call it a cafe affouch, an upside-down coffee, in one of those outside patios which line Dizingoff. At the table next to me was an older man, with a trimmed grey beard and beat-up black beret which was more working-class than bohemian. He wore a suit as these old-timers tended to but had, in a tip of the beret to the country where

1

he was now living, removed his tie. He had availed himself of the free newspapers which the cafe provided to its patrons-he had the Jerusalem Post, Haaretz, both in English, plus one in what I presumed to be Russian and another in Hebrew. It looked like he was going to make an afternoon of it. I did not begrudge him. I too had nursed many a coffee or beer for the better part of an afternoon in order to lengthen an enjoyable stay.

The cafe had those cylindrical sugar packets you often see in Europe and I had already poured a couple into my coffee and had ripped the opening of a third. I had seen him eying me and had the feeling he had been biting his tongue. That he had something he wanted to say.

My Hebrew was not that good but I had kind of figured out what the equivalent of 'why don't you have some coffee with your sugar was in Hebrew and so that was what I was expecting him to say when he finally addressed me.

But when he did address me, it was not in Hebrew but in a Russian accented English.

And what he said was "You should be shot for using so much sugar."

Which was funny. And would have been funny. Had he not been so serious. But I laughed anyway.

"If you don't mind me asking." He said, "what is it you do which allows you to be so generous with your sugar?"

We both knew the sugar packets were free. But we also both knew what he meant.

"I'm a writer," I said. I wasn't. But I could have been.

"A writer," he said "hoo whah. Well, Mr writer. If you have a few shekels to buy me a chocolate babka, I will tell you a story about sugar."

I had a few shekels.

This is the story he told me.

The rumour started at the chess club on Suvevorov Street. Not in the club, but on the roof of the four-story building that housed the club. A mid-March day had burst into double digits, Boris insisted it was 12 degrees, and tables, chairs and boards had been moved onto the roof in order to soak in the rare Moscow sun. Some of the men had taken off their shirts. All were men who should not be taking off their shirts even when showering or in the sauna. But it was 12 degrees and the sun was shining, Sicilian Defences were being played, Queens were being sacrificed and shirts were being discarded. Eventually, it was just Larianov and a man we knew only as The Bull for reasons which were not clear. Nothing in his physique, for he too had bared his torso, where dangled a gold star of David, would lead anyone to think it was an apt nickname. So we watched and kibitzed and insulted each others' play and flabby bodies until someone, it was probably Boris, it was nearly always Boris, said he heard there might be some sugar.

Both Larianov and The Bull stopped playing, even slapping down a meaty hand on the timer so no one would be penalized, and looked up at Boris demanding to know what he knew and where he had heard it from.

Like a fine piece of art, every rumour had its own provenance, often long and circuitous and complicated but, unlike a painting, which only needed one shady ownership to put the entire provenance in question, a rumour only needed one credible monger in its coterie to make it viable. In this case, it was Micha. Boris said he had heard it from Micha. Micha had a cousin who had a friend whose mother-in-law worked as a cleaning lady at a dacha, a summer house, on the Caspian Sea belonging to a Party member. It was not, all things considered, for a Russian rumour, that many degrees of separation, which gave us some optimism but mostly we were buoyed because it had come from Micha. Now Micha's average on rumours was still well below the Mendoza line - less than 1 in 5- but the key was he had been right about his last rumour, the raincoats. Now none of us had gotten a raincoat, though we had all stood in line, some of us for eight hours, mostly in an ironic pouring rain, but there was no question that there were raincoats to be had- we had seen people coming out of the store happily waving a washed-out red raincoat which from even where we were standing, back near the end of the line, we could see were clearly too small for the lucky recipient and would only fit a child, but they were raincoats nonetheless. But Micha had been right the last time and, in the rumour game, in the Russian rumour game, you were only as good as your last rumour, so now his sugar rumour, by way of Boris, carried a little bit more weight.

"I bet it is Bulgarian sugar," spat out Anton Mickeilovitch "I wouldn't feed Bulgarian sugar to my dog."

We all knew Anton Mickeilovitch did not own a dog and that he would likely give his left arm for a kilo of Bulgarian sugar but nobody pushed back because Anton Mickeilovitch had lost his wife and his brother in the last year and we all knew that even a kilo of sugar, Bulgarian or otherwise, could not sweeten his bitterness.

"Maybe it will be Latvian sugar," mused Larianov as he moved his knight to b7. This drew a hearty laugh from the crowd. Latvian sugar had near mythical aura about it. It was said that Khrushchev had built a factory just outside of Riga which produced such fine grains of sugar that they were like a Tahitian beach. Not a rat dropping ever made its way into the giant vats. His cook made him khvorost, angel wings of fried dough with powdered sugar, every night for dessert. None of us had ever seen it. None of us had tasted it. Had never known anyone who had seen it or tasted it. Even if it did exist, there was no way it would land into the hands of us patzers. Still, it was nice to dream.

No, if the rumour was true, and we were a long way from that, it would be Russian sugar. More brown than white. More pebble than grain. The factory was close to the Aral Sea which caused many people to say more salty than sweet.

In Moscow, nine out of the ten times we stood in a line, we did not know what we were standing in line for. Moscow was a city of people lining up for things. It did not matter what it was because it was surely something you needed. Because we needed everything. Or, at the very least, something you could trade for something you needed. Most of the time, you would get to the front of the line and they would have run out of the thing even before you knew what the thing was. Most of the time, you wouldn't get to the front of the line.

Boris's Misha rumour was of no use without knowing where this sugar would be distributed. Which store. Which stores. The sugar would surely not fall from the sky.

The sugar was the rumour.

The store. Well, the store was the information.

All the chess players on the roof understood that the rumour was as free as the air they breathed. They also understood that the information was no longer useful information if everyone knew about it. This was how it worked. They were not bitter. Even Anton Mickeilovitch, who could give the marror we ate on Passover a run for its money, was not bitter about it. Not more bitter than he already was. We knew there was a long line to wait in even before we could get to the line we would stand-in. If there was sugar and if there was really a location where it was being sold, the cleaning lady would know first and she would tell the people she would tell. They would then, in turn, tell the people they would tell. She would likely tell her son-in-law who would also tell the people he would tell and they the people they would tell. Maybe the son in law would tell his friend, Misha's cousin, and maybe then maybe Misha's cousin would tell Misha who in turn tell Boris. By then, a lot of people would be standing in line for what they hoped to be low-grade sugar the majority of the world would not feed to their dogs. While in line, but not a minute before, they would tell friends and family in the hope that when there would be another line they could say "hey remember when I told you about the sugar."

By the time Boris found out from Misha where the sugar was being distributed, there had been many more rumours. Everyone had a mother-in-law. Everyone had a cousin. Most of us had friends. Boris was my friend so I found out before he got in line but a long time after most of the rest of Moscow also got in line.

We knew after an hour there was no sugar. Not Latvian. Not Bulgarian. Not Russian. But an hour was not a long time and although we were not near the front, we were certainly not all the way in the back. And the sun was shining, a couple of us had brought our chess boards, and a couple of others had brought some vodka. This is only to say that when The Bull walked up and said he had heard a rumour about a line for tractor parts, nobody paid him much attention. We all lived in the city. None of us owned a tractor. And although we could maybe trade a tractor part for something else, we had pretty much decided to settle on the two sugars in the bush. So we all said no and returned to our games but then The Bull nudged me with his knee and said I should come with him to get a tractor part. And I said, I don't want a tractor part. And anyway, it is not a tractor part but a line for a tractor part. Then The Bull held up his own portable chess board and pieces and said "I will spot you a pawn and a bishop.

And I thought that was a strange thing to say because The Bull really hated to lose and although he was a much, much better player than me I was good enough to beat him if he spotted me a pawn and a bishop. So I went with him.

With that, the old Russian man drained his coffee and delicately wiped the chocolate babka crumbs from his beard and moustache. He had told this story before. This is where he paused for dramatic effect. I was ok with that. I didn't mind being a pawn in his game.

"Did you get a tractor part?" I asked.

He shook his head no.

"Sugar?" I liked this ending. That would have been my ending. Sugar at the tractor parts store. So classic.

But he shook his head no.

"So nu?" I asked, invoking the ancient Yiddish admonition

He smiled and said "Exit visa."

Exit visa.

"That's how you got out of the country?"

"Yes."

"And the tractor parts store?"

"Was the Brazilian consulate. The Bull, whose name was Meyer Meyerovitch, had heard a rumour of 20 exit visas. He was number 19 and I was 20."

"Good story," I said.

"You will write it?" He asked.

"Yes," I answered. "I will write it."

And now, nearly 30 years later, I have.

TWENTY CENT WINGS

Photograph © Brent Hofacker / 123rf.com

My uncle called me into his office. He did not look happy. He did not look happy at all. He had one bad eye so it was never clear if he was looking at you. But what I couldn't see, I could definitely feel.

He opened a folder, I could see it was my expense report folder, removed an item and pushed it in my direction.

"What is this?" he asked.

I picked it up and looked at it. It was a lunch receipt. From Gabby's Roadhouse in Brampton.

"I marked it down," I replied defensively. "It was lunch with Derek Dawson. You told me to take him to lunch."

Derek Dawson was the paint line supervisor for a huge manufacturer. We had been trying to get their account for years. I was the paint salesman in charge of the account.

My uncle snatched the receipt from me and inspected it carefully.

"I told you to take him to lunch. $6.99. What could you possibly eat for $6.99?"

"We shared chicken wings," I said. "Honey garlic. He said he liked honey garlic."

"Chicken wings?" My uncle looked like he was going to lose it. "It could be the biggest account in all of Ontario and you took him for chicken wings?"

"I asked him what he wanted. He said honey garlic chicken wings from Gabby's. We shared a dozen."

"You shared? You didn't even let him have his own plate?"

"Well the wings at Gabby's are really fat. I think that is why he likes them. Plus they come with fries. I only had four. Am sure he was full."

"$6.99?"

"It was 20-cent chicken wing day."

"20 cents for chicken wings." I was getting worried about my uncle. He had a heart condition.

"The Wednesday special."

"The Wednesday special?" Now he was only repeating what I was saying. He inspected the receipt again.

"You drank Coke?"

"Yes. We each had a Coke. Gabby's has free refills. He said he liked that."

"You couldn't have a beer?"

Salesmen all over the world were being berated for three martini lunches and I was about to be fired because I only drank Coke.

"$6.99? You submitted a receipt for $6.99?"

"I think I may have tipped $3. But I didn't expense it. I think I may have left a 10."

"$6.99. $6.99." My uncle couldn't get over it.

I was about to get fired for submitting too small an expense account.

"It was a good lunch." I was almost in tears. "We talked about fly fishing."

"Fly fishing?"

"Yeah. He likes to fish."

My uncle, for what I was sure was the first time in his life, was at a loss for words. Which was a good thing, because the next words out of his mouth would have been bad for me. But then the phone rang and there was a crisis in the lab and I slinked out of his office.

My uncle and my father both worked at Sherwin Williams in Montreal. It was a huge paint manufacturer. They were both chemical engineers. My father got out in the early 70s and got a job in Ottawa with the government. My uncle though stayed longer and he became one of the pioneers in developing a new dry paint, powder coating, application which was applied with an electrostatic charge and then baked in an oven. Unlike wet paint, which creates sludge which had to be disposed, the powder paint could be reused and recycled. At the late age of 50, my uncle decided to leave Sherwin Williams and open up his own company. He called it Protech Chemicals. He had two partners. Then one of his partners dropped out. My father came up with the money and became a small silent partner. He remained a very silent partner. My mom, however, would occasionally have something to say. Mostly asking her brother to give me my job back.

That kind of thing.

When I wrote, "Even though my uncle fired me three times, he was still my favorite uncle," my cousin David, who built the business with his father, was very quick to contact me in order to point out an error in that statement.

"David," I argued. "Your dad was my favorite uncle."

"Yes," he agreed. "I know he was."

"And I was fired three times," I continued.

And he said, "That is where I take issue."

I said, "Why?"

"Because," he explained, "you say you were fired three times. But you should have said you were ONLY fired three times."

Ah. Yes. He had a point. He had a good point. There are a bunch of examples. But I knew what he was talking about. He was talking about Ashley Broodmore.

Ashley Broodmore is not somebody's name. It is the name of a company. The company makes electrical boxes. We have all seen them. The grey boxes which house our fuses. But they made these big industrial electrical boxes. The ones you see in the back of a plant. They painted them with a grey paint. Many of the names of the paint colors we sold were crowned by my uncle and cousin. For example, the bright high-gloss orange paint we sold was called Philly Orange as an homage to the Philadelphia Flyers. My uncle, although a lifelong Montreal Canadiens fan, had a *joie de vivre* sense of humor.

The grey we sold Ashley Broodmore, however, had a name and designation which came straight from the electrical industry. It was called ASA 49 Grey.

It had many specifications. Durability, color, that kind of thing. One of the specifications was gloss. A lay person, one who buys paint for their wall, understands that a paint can either be matte, that is no or low gloss, or high gloss.

Ashley Broodmore's ASA 49 Grey had a specification of 35-39 gloss. Which is not quite matte and not quite gloss. And they had a high-fangled gloss meter to measure it when the pieces came out of the oven.

One day, the measurement was 41.

They halted production.

They called our office and said get somebody in here immediately.

That somebody was me.

Now the thing was, I didn't get the message right away.

Because my afternoon tennis game had gone into a third set.

So, by the time I retrieved my seven increasingly irritated messages, went home to shower and change into a suit, and drove the two hours to London, Ontario, it was already very late afternoon and the entire production line had been shut down for the entire day.

They were waiting for me in the conference room. The President and about 30 other people. I made my apologies, did not mention losing in a third set tiebreaker, and asked what I could do to help.

Someone handed me a piece of grey metal. It looked good. Perfect application.

"Do you have a gloss meter?"

I said I did. It was in the trunk of my Pontiac Phoenix. I went to the parking lot, opened my trunk, rummaged through the tennis rackets and balls, and retrieved it. I then went back to the conference room and did a reading.

41.

I asked for another piece.

41.

I asked for one more.

41.

"Forty one." I declared authoritatively. "Very consistent."

The President was not amused. "Our specs are 35-39," he said very firmly. "Your paint is off spec and it shut down our operation. Now what are you going to do about it?"

This was an easy one. We would manufacture a new batch overnight and ship it express the first thing in the morning.

It was a no-brainer.

Ashley Broodmore was a huge account.

It was a total no-brainer.

It was exactly what I should have said.

But I didn't.

Because I was in a bad mood.

I really hate losing in a third set tiebreaker.

And also driving two hours in rush hour to get dressed down over something that is not discernible to the naked eye. And about having to sell powder paint for a living.

So instead I said, "It's just an electrical box." To the President of the company who made electrical boxes and 30 of his employees.

He didn't say anything. I suspect he was in shock. I took the silence as a sign I could soldier on. "It is just an electrical box," I repeated. "It goes in the back of the plant. Nobody will ever be able to tell the difference."

The President nodded and thanked me for coming in. He then called my uncle and told him to never send me in ever again.

The most shocking part of the story is we didn't lose the account and I didn't lose my job.

Well, I did, but that was later.

I had written my first children's book by then and was devoting most of my time to what would become my first company. It wasn't really until I had my own company and my own lazy employees that I really understood my uncle.

So the third firing was the easiest. We both knew it was time.

Derek Dawson and I talked about fly fishing. I have never fished but I had read a few books. *A River Runs Through It*. Also, as you may have already guessed, I can spin a tale. I never really liked talking about paint. I would drop by the plant, he would take a cigarette break and we would stand outside near the loading docks and talk about fishing. Which lure to use. Which were the best fishing spots. We never mentioned paint. I discovered that selling was about connecting with people.

I was good at that.

It was the biggest account I ever landed. The competition never had a chance after that.

Go figure.

Fly fishing.

I actually got a few big accounts that year.

"We had a good year," I said to my uncle.

"6.99," he retorted. I would like to think he was joking. But I don't really think so. He knew I was just phoning it in. Just biding my time. I can't really blame him.

Selling paint was not my thing. I went on to discover other things. I am still discovering.

We got along much better when we were just uncle and nephew. We played poker. I took him shopping. Then back to return the things he had bought. I let him pick the restaurants. My choices were always shit.

We complained about employees. We reminisced about customers. About sales trips. About the time he told the not-pregnant Lisa that smoking was not good for the baby. I boasted about my sales, my numbers, my successes. I picked up the check.

I call my cousin David while I am writing this story and ask how much we used to sell the ASA 49 Grey for.

We.

25 years later, and I am still saying "we."

Fired three times and I am still saying "we."

"You writing the Ashley Broodmore story?" he asks. I say, "Yeah."

"It's just an electrical box."

"Yeah, I dunno. Kinda sounds like something I might have said."

"You were so bad."

"I know. So bad. At least it produced some good stories."

"You tell the chicken wing story?"

"Yeah," I reply.

"Derek Dawson." He remembers the name right away.

"I'm impressed," I say.

"Are you fucking kidding me! Gabby's Roadhouse. $6.99."

"It was a monster account," I say.

"Yes," he agrees. "It was a monster."

"Free Coke refills," I say.

"You ever fish with Derek Dawson?" I didn't answer. He knew I didn't.

"Classic story. You wrote it up?"

"Yeah."

"Send it to me."

So I do. I don't hear back but a few days later a FedEx arrives at my house. I open it up and there are three loonies—three dollars—and a note.

It is from my cousin David.

"This covers the tip."

The last meal I had alone at a restaurant with my uncle was at a roadside joint in Hallandale Florida called Big Daddy Flanigan's. It was a liquor store which doubled as a type of diner. Ribs, burgers. That kind of thing. It was a dive and it wasn't clear why he liked it, but he insisted it was good. We had gone on some sort of wild goose chase looking for a $99 suit he had heard advertised on TV. We stopped at Flanigan's for lunch on the way back. We both had beers and I ordered the fish tacos. My uncle looked sideways at the waitress. I think he was trying to read her name tag.

"Justine," I said out loud.

"Let me ask you this, Justine," said my uncle. "Do you have 20-cent wings?" he said it with a straight face.

Justine was unfazed.

"$9.99 for a dozen," she replied.

"It comes with fries?"

"Yes, sir."

"Okay. I will have wings."

"Which flavor would you like?"

"Do you have honey garlic?"

Justine said yes.

"Okay. A dozen honey garlic."

Justine left. I looked over at my uncle. His face did not betray a thing.

Then he slowly lifted his Corona. It was really only a few inches above the table.

"To Derek Dawson," he said.

"To Derek Dawson," I replied.

THE BLESSING

Photograph © Lisa Young / 123rf.com

Sometimes when I try a dropshot in pickleball and it doesn't make it over the net, my sister-in-law will say, "Serves you right." As if I have been punished by God for trying such a sneaky shot. When she reads this story from back in the day, she will no doubt also say that it serves me right. That I flew too close to the sun. She will look up from her paperback—she does not like eBooks—wag her finger at me, and say it serves me right. She will be smiling but she will mean it. I will say, "Why does it serve me right?" And she will say because I tried to date two women on the same day. And I will say that's not what happened. And she will say it sure sounds like that is what happened.

Icarus and I, both misunderstood.

Aviva Blatt was one of the women. She was beautiful. She was smart. She was accomplished. She also possessed a quality which I was finding to be increasingly rare—she liked me. We had gone out twice. Once to Kalendar with a K and once to play mini putt. Now Aviva Blatt had invited me to her family's house for Shabbat—Saturday—lunch. She had done it in a manner which I considered to be a little underhanded. She had called me and asked if I were free for lunch on Saturday. I told her yes, I was wide open, I had no plans, my schedule was totally unmarred by appointments. I was. She said, "Great, you will come for Shabbat lunch at my parent's house."

You see.

Underhanded.

If she had led with, 'Do you want to come for Shabbat lunch?' I would have then rapidly but calmly accessed my excuse folder. I had dozens. Some were even virgin excuses. Never used before.

But now all I could say was, "Sounds great. Looking forward to it."

I called Allie.

I said, "I have a situation."

She said, "Your life is a situation."

"Aviva Blatt has invited me to her parents' house for Shabbat lunch."

She said, "That's your situation?"

I said, "Yeah."

She said, "Let me get this straight. A beautiful woman who you like and, and I can't stress this part too much, who likes you, has invited you to lunch at her parents' house and you believe this is a situation?"

I said, "Yes. I do. I might suggest this could even be considered a code red."

Allie said, "I can't wait to hear this."

And I said, "They are going to ask me to lead *Birkat*."

"They are going to ask you to lead *Birkat*?"

"Yes. *Birkat Hamazon*. The prayer after the meal."

Allie said, "I know what *Birkat Hamazon* is, idiot."

I said, "Well, you used a question mark."

She said, "I was just questioning as to why they were going to ask you to lead it."

"They will. It is an honor they bestow on guests. They are definitely going to ask me."

"Maybe they will have other guests."

"I'm sure they will have other guests. But I am going to be the motherfucking guest of honor."

I don't know why I was getting angry at Allie.

"You could say no."

"How is that going to look? You know I can't say no."

"Okay. So suck it up. I don't really know what the problem is. You have no problem speaking, even singing in front of crowds. You revel in it."

I said, "You don't know what the problem is?"

And she said, "No."

So I said, "I will tell you what the problem is. The problem is I don't know *Birkat Hamazon*."

"You don't?"

I said, "No."

"You didn't say it at home?"

I said, "No. My father did the prayers before the meal. The blessing on the wine. The blessing on the bread. We never did the prayer after the meal."

"You never went to Hebrew school?"

I said, "No."

"You never went to camp?"

I said, "You know I never went to camp."

"But you have lots of religious friends. You go to Shabbat lunch at their house all the time. What do you do at the Pratzers' or Rosens'?"

"What do I do? I sit there like a schmuck. I look at my watch. Every once in a while I bang the table."

"You don't know any of it?"

"I know a few words here and there. I certainly don't know how to lead it."

"Well," she said. "You know what you have?"

I said, "What?"

She said, "You, sir, have got yourself a situation."

I didn't say anything.

She continued, "It's only Thursday."

I said, "I know."

She said, "Saturday is still two days away."

I said, "Tell me more, Professor Science."

She said, "Do you really think it is a good idea to make fun of the one person who stands in the way of what will surely be a day of abject humiliation?"

I figured that was a rhetorical question. "Are you going to help me?!"

"Look, the only part you need to know is the beginning. It is a call and response. Then the whole group joins in. I will record it for you on a cassette."

"What about the other part?"

"You don't need to know it. Some of it is even silent prayer. If you want, every once in a while, you can throw in a '*ha rachaman*.' It comes up a lot."

"*Ha rachaman?*"

"Yeah. Come pick it up in an hour. You can play it in your car and memorize it. You can do this."

"You really think I can?"

She said, "Not really, but it will make a good story. I will see you soon."

I said, "Thanks."

She said, "You owe me."

The other woman was Tamara Blankenstein. Lewberg and I ran into her at Yorkdale Mall the Friday before my Shabbat lunch. He called and said he wanted to buy new tennis shoes. I said, "Lewberg, you don't play tennis." And he said, "I never had the right shoes." So I picked him up. He got in the car and said, "What the fuck are we listening to?" I popped out Allie's cassette tape of the Hebrew blessing I had been trying to memorize and replaced it with Van Morrison.

"Aviva Blatt," I said.

"Lunch tomorrow?"

I said, "Yeah."

"Birkat Hamazon?"

I said, "Yeah."

He said, "Jesus. Seems like a lot of work."

Lewberg bought three pair of tennis shoes because he couldn't decide which pair he was never ever going to wear and we ran into Tamara Blankenstein at the checkout. Lewberg knew her better than I, and we made small talk for a few minutes.

She was also beautiful and smart and accomplished. She was really nice but was a little bit too Birkenstock and granola for me. Even if I had not been dating Aviva Blatt, I'm not sure I would have wanted to go out with her. But that turned out to be a moot point because she did not want to go out with me.

I know this because Lewberg called me later in the day and said, "She doesn't want to go out with you."

I said, "You are going to have to narrow it down a little. That's a pretty long list."

And he said, "Tamara Blankenstein. She doesn't want to go out with you." Lewberg seemed like he was enjoying telling me his news.

"She doesn't want to go out with me?"

"No."

"How do you know she doesn't want to go out with me?"

"Because," he said patiently, "after we ran into her in the mall, I called and asked her."

"If she wanted to go out with me?"

"Yes."

"Tamara Blankenstein?"

"Yes."

"We ran into her at the mall and then you called her and asked if she wanted to go out with me?"

"Yes," he said "she doesn't, by the way."

"Lewberg," I was trying to control my temper, "why would you call Tamara Blankenstein and ask her if she wanted to go out with me?"

"Because you said she was cute."

"I said she was cute?"

"Yes."

"Lewberg, why would you think that me saying she was cute meant I wanted you to call her and ask if she wanted to go out with me?"

Lewberg was quiet for a second and said, "Because that's what friends do."

It was hard to get angry at Lewberg. He was a loyal friend. He was a people-pleaser. Not for a second did he think he had done anything wrong.

I said, "But you know I am dating Aviva Blatt."

Lewberg said, "Hey, Pappy, I don't judge. Anyway, there is no issue because she doesn't want to go out with you. It's all good."

Well, it really wasn't all good, but there was no point trying to explain it to Lewberg, who now said, "Want to meet at the Firkin for a drink?"

I said, "Hold on. Why doesn't she want to go out with me?"

And Lewberg said, "Does it matter?"

And I said, "I suppose not." And I guess it didn't. "I will meet you there in 15." But Lewberg had already hung up.

He was already sitting at the patio with what appeared to be his second Ketel and cranberry in his hand and a Guinness in front of my seat.

"Why doesn't she want to go out with me?" I asked before taking my first sip.

"Who?"

"Tamara Blankenstein. Why doesn't she want to go out with me?"

"I thought we had settled this."

I said, "No."

Lewberg took a big gulp of his drink and motioned the waitress for another.

He shrugged his shoulders and said, "Do you really want to do this?"

I said, "She wasn't attracted to me?"

Lewberg said, "That was the obvious one. That would have been my guess. But no. She said she had no problem with you physically."

"She had no problem with me physically?"

"No."

"Not exactly a glowing review, but I guess better than revulsion. Okay. My personality?"

"That was my second guess. But no, she said you were funny and charming. Which makes me question her sanity."

"So what the fuck?"

Lewberg said, "She thought you were a little too Jewish."

"Too Jewish?"

"Yup."

"Tamara Blankenstein?"

"Yes."

"Tamara Blankenstein whose grandfather was Rabbi Blankenstein. That Tamara Blankenstein?"

"Yes."

"She said I was a little too Jewish?"

He said, "Yes."

I said, "I eat pepperoni pizza."

Lewberg said, "I know. I have eaten it with you."

"I mix milk and meat."

Lewberg said, "I know."

I said, "I don't go to synagogue and don't fast on Yom Kippur."

Lewberg said, "You don't have to convince me. You are a shit Jew."

"So what then?"

Lewberg said, "You used the phrase."

I said, "I used the phrase?"

"Yes. When she asked you how your sister in Israel was, you said, '*Baruch Hashem.*'"

I said, "I said *Baruch Hashem*?"

"Yes," said Lewberg. "Praise the Lord."

"Lewberg," I said calmly. "I know what *Baruch Hashem* means. Why is saying that an issue?"

"She dated Joel Mandlebaum. He became a little too religious for her. She said she respected his beliefs but didn't want to go through that again."

"Joel Mandlebaum?"

"Yeah. One minute he's a bacon double cheeseburger guy and the next he is going to pray three times a day."

I said, "I like Joel Mandlebaum."

Lewberg said, "Me too. Great putter. But he became a bit too religious for her."

"Lewberg," I said, "I'm not becoming more religious. If anything, I am becoming less religious."

"She said she got the impression you were on a path."

"A path? I'm not on a path!"

Lewberg said, "You are preaching to the converted. But you know, *Baruch Hashem*."

I said, "I was using it ironically."

Lewberg said, "I know."

"You didn't explain I was using it ironically?"

"Hey. I made the call. It's not on me to get into semantics with her. That's on you. I mean, it's your path."

There wasn't much to say after that. Lewberg wasn't going to be convinced, and anyway, I had a Shabbat lunch at the Blatts' the next day.

So I forgot about it.

For about an hour.

I phoned Goldfarb in order to tell him I was going to call in a marker. Am not crazy about having to call Goldfarb and having to call in a marker. I'd rather take a marker to my grave. It's like in golf when you use your mulligan on the second hole. " Am using my mulligan here," you announce. Everyone nods and takes note. Then you play like shit for the rest of the round because of the pressure, knowing you have already used your mulligan and have no more mulligans to use. Or you can be like Lewberg, who announces, "I'm going to use my mulligan here," even though we all know he used it three holes ago.

So I wasn't thrilled about using a marker up with Goldfarb, but it was what it was.

Goldfarb picked up the phone on the fourth ring.

I said, "I am going to call in a marker."

Goldfarb quickly replied, "You don't have a marker with me." But we both knew that's bullshit. So I didn't say anything.

There was silence for a few seconds and then Goldfarb said, "This makes us even?"

I said, "Yes." I didn't say that friends don't keep favor ledgers with friends. Because I knew there was no point. That is how Goldfarb operates. He is a great friend. But you can't leave his house without paying your backgammon losses. That is just how it is.

He said, "What do you need?"

"Tamara Blankenstein."

"Tamara Blankenstein?"

I said, "Yeah. I want to go out with her and tell her I am not on a path."

"You want to go out with her and tell her you are not on a path?"

I said, "Yes."

Goldfarb said, "Am I supposed to know what that means?"

I said, "It doesn't matter. Can you help me?"

Goldfarb said, "Aren't you dating Aviva Blatt?"

I said, "We have gone out twice. Am going to her parents' house for Shabbat lunch tomorrow."

Goldfarb said, "*Birkat Hamazon*?"

I said, "Yeah."

He said, "How is that going?"

I said, "I have it down cold. Have been listening to it endlessly in my car."

"But now you want to go out with Tamara Blankenstein?"

"I don't want to go 'out' out with her. I just want to go out with her to tell her I am not on a path."

"You want to use up a marker for that?" asked Goldfarb.

I said, "Yes."

Goldfarb said, "You know I have a marker with Tamara Blankenstein."

I said, "I know."

"Because of that thing."

I said, "I know."

He said, "Let me see what I can do."

I call Tamara Blankenstein. She was expecting my call. Goldfarb did his part. We have a very nice conversation. I tell her about pepperoni pizza. She tells me about Joel Mandlebaum. I say she doesn't have to explain. I get it. We do a little Seinfeld 'not that there is anything wrong with it.' We arrange to go out for dinner on Saturday night. I suggest shellfish. Lobster. Shrimp. She says great.

Aviva Blatt's mom is a great cook. Chopped liver. Matzo ball soup. Brisket. Roast potatoes. I think she is anyway, because I don't really eat all that much because I am nervous about the blessing. I move food around my plate and then move more when my refusals for seconds go unheeded. Aviva whispers, "Eat something," and I do my best to put some food away. I feel a little sick. I'm not sure if throwing up is worse than not eating. I think both are bad. Anyway, it doesn't matter because I am about to rock this blessing.

But then Aviva Blatt's mother says:

"And now our guest of honor, my brother Haim, who came all the way from New York, is going to lead us in the *Birkat Hamazon*."

Wait what?

Uncle Haim?

Uncle Haim is the motherfucking guest of honor?

Did Mrs. Blatt just call an audible because I didn't eat her brisket?

I am encouraged to sing with the rest but I haven't studied that part. I mostly sit like a schmuck and bang the table. Once I try a 'ha rachaman,' but it turns out to be during the silent prayer. Am pretty sure I am not getting invited back. News of my pepperoni pizza past must have filtered back. Aviva Blatt does not look happy. She does not look happy at all.

I am not a big date planner. Shower. Nose hair trim. Brush my teeth. Mouthwash.

But I spend a lot of time thinking of the music I am going to play in the car. It sets the tone. It sets the mood. It tells the woman the type of guy I am.

I had thought about it and settled on the Grateful Dead. I didn't really like the Grateful Dead. I didn't even own any Grateful Dead. I had to stop at Lewberg's and borrow a cassette from him. But at the last minute I changed my mind. It would look like I was trying too hard. My friend Ezekial had taught me to stick with the tried and true. That would be Grover Washington Junior's *Just the Two of Us*. I popped the Dead out, rummaged through my console and snapped in the new cassette. But, in my haste, I must have grabbed the wrong cassette.

So when Tamara Blankenstein slid into the front seat, she was not greeted by the dulcet tones of Bill Withers.

No.

Instead she was greeted by Allie's lovely voice, reciting the blessing after the meal.

Rabotai Nevarech.

Allie has only recorded the opening. She has it on a loop.

We listen to it a few times.

Shame. I really had it down cold.

Tamara Blankenstein asks me to take her home. She doesn't even wave goodbye.

I don't blame her.

Allie's recording was a little pitchy.

The Live at Budokan version is much better.

THE KOTEL

Photograph © Moshe / Lakewood Fogels

When Harold heard I was going to Israel to visit my sister, he asked if I could bring something for him. Now Harold and I have been friends for a long time, and he is well-aware of my no-shlepping rule, so I knew he wasn't going to saddle me with a big package. Truth be told, I knew he wasn't going to saddle me with any package at all. So I was pretty confident when I walked into his house. My confidence was not unfounded, because he directed me to a small folded piece of paper which lay on the kitchen table. I immediately knew what it was for, and I quickly told him I didn't think I would be going to Jerusalem this time.

He said, "Take it just in case."

I said, "Okay."

My brother, sister-in-law, and youngest niece, Rena, were going to Israel in order to visit my sister and her family.

My sister lives in the town of Ramat Beit Shemesh. It is an Anglo-Orthodox town located almost midway between Tel Aviv and Jerusalem. I say Anglo because most of the inhabitants are former Americans, Canadians, Brits, and South Africans. There are native-born Israelis, but it is predominantly families who immigrated to Israel—made aliyah—from elsewhere. Many, not all, are also former secular Jews who then became more religious later in their lives. My sister and brother-in-law fit into that category. It is said one can gauge the type of Jew you are by your choice of head covering. My brother-in-law and his sons and sons-in-law all wear black hats. They are strictly kosher and pray three times a day.

I don't cover my head and enjoy the occasional cheeseburger.

But despite our differences, we are a very close family.

We were staying at a hotel in Tel Aviv and the plan was to split up our time between the beach and visiting our family.

We arrived on a Tuesday and we all dined together on Wednesday night, on Thursday night, and then spent the entire Sabbath at their house in Ramat Beit Shemesh. Friday night dinner. Saturday lunch. Saturday dinner.

It was fantastic!

My sister is a great cook and hanging out with my nephews, nieces, and their respective babies was a real treat.

My sister is an actual bonafide matchmaker and has quite the reputation in her town. Neighbors dropped by all day in order to greet the 'brothers from America.'

Let me say it again—it was fantastic!

But, much like the famed scene in *The Frisco Kid*, by the end of the day on Saturday, the sun couldn't set fast enough for us.

We said our goodbyes and took a taxi back to our hotel in Tel Aviv.

Sunday was a pool and beach day. We rented bikes and ambled down the 'Tayelet,' the Tel Aviv beach promenade. We texted with my sister and the kids during the day but mostly just to touch base.

We ended the day on the beach with olives and hummus and a cold Israeli beer.

Rena asked if we were going to see the family that night, but it looked like we would have a night alone. We really didn't feel like going back to Ramat Beit Shemesh.

We threw out the idea of meeting in Tel Aviv for dinner, but although Tel Aviv was but 40 minutes away, my sister had only been five times in 15 years.

"Why would I go to Tel Aviv?" she would say. I knew what she meant. Tel Aviv was the center of secular non-religious life in Israel. It was easier to find a kosher restaurant in Toronto.

So we knew our offer was akin to a Yom Kippur lunch invitation.

But then my brother and I began to feel guilty.

"If you want, we'll meet you in Jerusalem for dinner."

It was 8:00, we hadn't showered, and Jerusalem was an hour away.

Now you have to understand. Three of the kids had babies. My sister didn't like to leave the house at the best of times. Only one of them even had a car.

So, it was mostly just a bluff.

My niece Shoshanah was the first to call the bluff.

She texted, "The Marcuses are in! We will take the train."

Then Ariel said, "Okay, Jerusalem sounds fun."

Then Natan said, "Us too. We might be a little late."

Then Ben, Ben who had two babies who already should have been in bed, who was careful and deliberate, said, "We just ordered a taxi."

Now although my sister is loath to leave the house, certainly at this hour, she is stricken by a greater affliction.

FOMO.

Fear of missing out.

So her text, "We're also on our way," did not come as a surprise.

Rena was thrilled. My sister-in-law, to her credit, was a real sport. "It will be an adventure," she said.

We jumped in a taxi of our own and made our way to Jerusalem.

It was a little after 10:00 when we made it to Mamilla Mall—the shopping and restaurant mall just outside the gates of the Old City.

Fearing we might not get a taxi to get home, I threw down some bills and asked our driver if he wouldn't might waiting. I said we wouldn't be long.

We were a big group. We sent out a team to try to secure a table for 12. The Italian restaurant seemed perfect, but Ben wanted to first talk to their kashrut supervisor to make sure it was at their level of kosher. My brother gives me a look. He is going to faint from hunger. Luckily my brother-in-law arrives and gives the thumbs-up. We can eat here.

Our waitress is Tali. My sister begins to pepper her with questions. "What does it come with?" "Can I substitute this?" My brother bangs his head on the table. I decide to take over. I order multiple pizzas, pastas, and salads. I over-order.

"Ronnie, that is way too much," argues my sister.

"Who will take leftovers home?" I ask.

Everyone raises their hands.

Dinner is great, but it is now midnight. I am worried about the taxi driver. I dial the number, but Natan takes my phone.

"Achi—my brother—" he says. "This is Gingi—he uses the Hebrew term for redhead—we are going to be a little late. Beseder? Okay?"

The taxi driver says, "Eyn bayot. No problem."

We are too full for dessert. Leftovers are being packaged. Babies being once again rocked to sleep. It was a bonus dinner manufactured from whole cloth. You can say what you want, but you just can't beat family.

It is late. We are exhausted. We still have an hour ride back to Tel Aviv. But it was worth it.

We begin to say our goodbyes, and then my sister shocks the hell out of me by saying, "We have to go to the Kotel." The Wailing Wall. The Western Wall. It is the holiest and most revered place in all of Judaism.

I say, "What?"

My sister calmly says, "You can't go to Jerusalem without going to the Kotel."

I say, "It is 12:30 am."

But Rena says, "She's kinda right, Uncle Ronnie. You can't go to Jerusalem without going to the Kotel."

Everyone agrees.

I hand the phone to Natan.

He calls the taxi driver.

"Achi," he says, "it is Gingi. Tishma, listen, we are going to the Kotel." They are now talking like old friends. The taxi driver says he isn't going anywhere.

So the 12 of us, pushing baby carriages through the narrow cobblestone streets of the Armenian Quarter, make our way to the Kotel.

We turn the corner, past the old ladies selling red thread to ward off the evil eye, and there it is.

The Kotel.

And the courtyard is packed. It is teeming with people.

Black hats.

Knit kippas.

Baseball caps.

No hats.

Everyone goes to say a prayer.

I am not religious.

I don't pray.

But now I remember my friend Harold has given me a note to slip in between the cracks in the wall. The Jewish equivalent of throwing coins into Trevi Fountain. I had forgotten about it, and between seeing my family and being in Tel Aviv, we hadn't been to Jerusalem. I push my way through the throngs of men who are swaying back and forth in deep prayer and find myself in front of the wall. This ancient wall which was said to have been some part of the old temple. I pull out my wallet and find the note. The cracks in front of me are already full of notes. I don't know what becomes of them. I guess they get gathered every morning and sent to some rabbis. I really don't know.

Anyway, I don't really want Harold's note to get mixed up with the others. He has MS. He is in a wheelchair. I mean, I don't really believe in this stuff, but I am here. My sister's stubbornness has put me right here.

I see a crack, but it is out of my reach. I turn to two black-hat-cladded men, really just boys, praying next to me. One catches my eye and I point to the crack. I try to formulate a request in Hebrew in my head but I don't have to. Within five seconds, I am given a boost. Like the boost I used to get to sneak over the wall into the public pool back in Montreal. I slip in the note and start to thank the boosters but they have resumed their prayers.

My family regroups.

I say, "Can we go now?"

My sister says, "Now we can go."

The taxi driver and Natan hug.

We all want to sleep in the car, but the taxi driver announces he has cataracts. He doesn't usually drive at night.

I volunteer to stay up and guide him back to Tel Aviv.

Truth is, I am no longer all that tired. I am a little wired. I might have a touch of Jerusalem Fever.

Shoshanah texts the next day, "Thanks, Uncle Ronnie and Uncle Dov. Best night ever!"

She is not wrong.

Back in Toronto, I invite myself for lunch at Harold's house. They have hummus and olives. I tell him I delivered his note. I tell him I slipped it into one of the higher cracks.

"Closer to God," he says. But I know he is mocking me.

"So what was in the note?" I ask. "Or is it like a birthday wish?"

He is smiling now. His wife, Gili, is laughing.

I wait. And then he tells me.

"The note was blank. I just wanted to get you to the Kotel."

GLORY DAYS

My friend Harold Rosen has a son called Jacob. He is a good kid. You should have seen the face he made when I told him I was once the star of my high school basketball team.

I wish I could say it was a look of surprise.

It wasn't.

I wish I could say he was incredulous.

But I can't.

His expression did not rise to the level of incredulity.

To be clear:

I wasn't saying I had played in the NBA with Kareem Abdul Jabbar.

I wasn't saying I had once beaten Michael Jordan in a game of one-on-one.

I only said I was once the star of my high school basketball team.

High school.

Jacob could not conceive of me ever being young. Let alone the notion I had once donned a pair of high tops and flew through the air to delicately deliver the ball into the basket with my patent finger roll.

But I was.

And I did.

I played on my high school basketball team, Ridgemont High School in Ottawa, Canada, in Grade 10 and 11. That is not where I was a high school basketball star.

I can imagine my friend Steve Koobs Kahansky reading this part. He has started smiling to himself because he knows what is coming up. His wife, Karen, asks what is so funny. He will say something he just read. But he means something he is about to read. But he doesn't even have to read it. He knows I can't write about playing basketball at Ridgemont without telling the story about the time I scored on my own basket.

In Grade 10, I made the basketball team by the skin of my teeth. I was the eleventh guy on a 10-person squad. The coach, Coach Keene, liked me. "Zeevy," he would say, "I like your hustle." Not enough to get me in the game. But he liked my hustle.

The second-stringers played when we were up by 40 points or down by 40 points. And we were never up by 40 points. I played, well, let's just say waiting for the Messiah is more hopeful.

One game, we were playing against our arch-rivals, Canterbury High School. Our family actually lived on Canterbury Street and the school was very close by. But my parents chose Ridgemont because they heard it had another Jew.

I wish I was joking.

It was a home game and the stands were full because there was going to be a sock hop after the game.

A sock hop.

Again, I wish I was joking.

I called Canterbury our arch-rival but that kind of implies that we won the occasional game.

We didn't.

Ever.

When we played in their gym, they would come out of the locker room to the sound of a song called Basketball Jones.

Many of the stories I tell I remember only in the telling. But I remember Basketball Jones as if it were yesterday.

It was by Cheech and Chong.

How Canterbury High School allowed the theme song to come from that famed, pot-smoking, Dave's Not Here duo, I'll never know. But the song came on, blasting, the Canterbury team would come strutting out, and we never had a chance.

Tonight's game however, was at our gym. We wouldn't have to deal with a song, only the vastly superior Canterbury basketball players.

It wasn't long before we were down by 40. Our 10-strong team took turns being sacrificial lambs. And then, out of the blue, the Coach calls out, "Zeevy, get in there."

Am not sure if any of you played a sport in high school. Am not sure any of you were a never-used, fourth-string scrub who never played. If not, let me explain: when you are a never-used, fourth-string scrub, your mind has a tendency to wander. A cute girl in the stands. Cheech and Chong. World peace.

And so I got in the game without having as complete a picture of the situation as I might have had were I not contemplating world peace. So when our center miraculously won the tip on the far side of the court and nudged it into my surprised and willing hands, I proceeded to deftly dribble through and around two or three helpless and befuddled Canterbury players all the way to the basket on the other side of court, where I gently laid it into the basket using the aforementioned finger roll.

The only thing:

It was into my own basket.

Sitting on the bench, you see, I neglected to notice which way we were going.

And so, I scored into my own basket.

In front of what looked to be the entire school.

Earning myself the moniker, one which stayed with me for the rest of the year of Wrong-Way Zevy.

In Grade 11, I got to play more. We didn't beat Canterbury. I'm not sure we beat anyone. But I got to play. And I got better. And I became a bit of a basketball fanatic. We had two practices a day, and I even used to listen to the college games on shortwave radio.

On the radio.

Like I said, I was a bit of a fanatic.

So by the time my father called a family meeting, spread out a map of the world and pointed to a spot in Southeast Asia—the city state of Singapore—where we would be spending the next two years—I was pretty into basketball.

I would be spending my last two years of high school at the United World College of South East Asia. It was an international school with a mix of rich, local Chinese, Indonesian, and Malaysian students, plus expatriates from around the world.

It was an international school, but it was English in tone and demeanor. There was a school uniform and we would be studying for English A-levels. The two big sports were soccer and rugby. In both, our school were local powerhouses.

On week one I discovered, much to my chagrin and dismay, that there was no school basketball team.

The head of sport was Mr. Steele. I went to see him. He gave me the once-over. He did not like what he saw. He was especially not a fan of my afro.

"I'm afraid we don't offer a school basketball team, Mr. Zevy." He couldn't wait to get me out of his office. But at least he pronounced my name correctly.

"Can I ask you why not?" I don't have a clear picture of myself as a 16 year old, but I have no trouble hearing the words of my argumentative 16-year-old niece, Rena.

"Mr. Zevy. Our school plays football and rugby. This is an English school."

It wasn't.

"Our students don't play basketball."

He made basketball sound like leprosy.

"I am sure there are some students who play basketball."

"Perhaps. But we have no one here on staff who is able, interested, or capable of teaching basketball."

Again he made basketball sound like an infectious disease.

"I could coach," I said.

He looked up from his desk for the first time and looked me in the eye. "You?"

Here, in case you were wondering, was a legitimate example of incredulity.

"Yes. I know the University of North Carolina playbook off by heart."

"The University of North Carolina?"

It looked like he might have a stroke.

"Yes," I said, "the Tar Heels."

Although, seems unlikely I said that.

I may have been impudent, but I wasn't crazy.

"The University of North Carolina?" he said now for the second time.

"Yes. They use a lot of backdoor cuts."

I'm now just making shit up. There is no way I ever said that.

"You are going to coach?"

"Mr. Steele. I want to play basketball. There must be competition with other schools like there is in soccer and rugby."

"There is," he said. "With some of the local schools and the American school."

"Okay, then. You get us on the schedule and I will get us a team."

And then he did something really weird and unexpected. He shrugged his shoulders and said, "Okay."

There were no tryouts for the 1976 UWCSEA basketball team. A basketball team needs five players to compete in a game.

I found six:

Myself

Kevin O'Kane from Canada

Rob Prester from the US

Nim Asukal from Thailand

David Tow from Australia

and Alon Wegner from Israel.

We were fast. We had some good outside shooters.

But we had no height.

We needed a center.

Then one day, during our third practice, Moses Temo walked into the gym. Moses was the six-foot-four star of the rugby team from the Polynesian island of Fiji.

We were doing layup drills. He just stood there for a few minutes while we practiced our layups. Then an errant ball rolled to his feet. He tossed it back using the two-handed rugby motion.

"You play?" I asked.

He shook his head no.

And then he said, "No, but, how hard could it be."

There you have it.

The UWCSEA basketball team.

We were good.

We started winning games.

We started getting fans.

Parents started coming to games. Not my parents. But parents. Nim Asukal's dad would come with a Super 8 camera.

Then one day, out of the blue, cheerleaders appeared. With actual girls!

Finally it was time to play the dreaded American School. They were the Canterbury HS of Singapore. They were undefeated. They had three coaches. They had more than two practice balls.

The stands were full.

I started hearing catcalls.

At first I couldn't make it out but then it became clearer. They were calling me Tumbleweed. Because of my hair.

"Hey, Tumbleweed."

Followed by a disparaging and anatomically impossible request of my mother.

"Hey, Tumbleweed."

The name of my publishing company is now Tumbleweed Press.

Anyway, they thought they were insulting me. They had no idea how much better Tumbleweed was than Wrong-Way.

I scored 22 that day. We were outclassed, but we fought tooth and nail. We were down one when Moses got fouled with two seconds to go.

Moses had not made a foul shot all season. He made Shaquille O'Neil look like Rick Barry.

I remember taking my shirt off.

I remember not looking up.

If I had, I would have seen Moses Temo bank two back-to-back free throws off the backboard for a 43-42 win.

Bruce Springsteen sings about Glory Days. It's just a song.

I tell myself it's just a song.

But that win against the American School might have been my crowning moment. Maybe not in my life, but certainly in my basketball career.

22 points.

My friend Phil asks if I heard about the reunion. I say I haven't. He says there is a Facebook page. I tell him I am not on Facebook. I met Phil in Singapore. We were in the same history class. We became best friends. I was best man at his wedding. He says he is going to check it out. I say it is depressing to see how old we have all gotten. But then I get curious and set up a page. I was right. Everyone looks like shit. I must look like shit, too. I have an old photo album and I upload the pictures. Others share pictures. It is honestly a bit surreal. We have jumped from 16 to 60. The irony is there are so many years to fill, but we get caught up in a matter of a few sentences. It is fun, but it is short-lived. What's the line from the Big Chill? "We knew each other for a short time a long time ago." Something like that.

Nice to hear from Kevin O'Kane. He is a mining executive in Western Canada. He was a Philadelphia Flyers fan. He loved Bobby Clarke. Has anyone heard from Moses, I ask. Yes, his sister Terry, who dated him in high school is still in contact. I reach out, but I don't hear back. People are busy I guess. I move from checking for messages six times a day to once a day and then to once a week. It has played itself out. And then I get a message from Nim Asukal. I wish I remembered him better, but I don't. He was very quiet. He rarely took a shot but played great defence. His glasses would get knocked off his face about five times a game.

The message is short. "Hey Ron, I thought you would enjoy this." There is an attachment. It is a video clip. It is short and very grainy. It is mostly of Nim. He has his hands raised high, playing man-to-man defence. It kind of looks like a man giving himself up to the authorities. It makes sense. The video was taken by his father after all. But then the ball gets turned over and we are on offence. Someone is dribbling the ball. You can't see his face. But the afro is unmistakeable. Then the video cuts out for a second and cuts back just in time to see the layup. It is a finger roll.

I watch it again.

Then again.

Then I attach it to an email.

I scan through my contacts until I find it.

Jacob Rosen.

Take that, you punk!

SCHWARTZMAN'S

Goldfarb and I were starving. We were sitting at my pool, doing our best not to ruin our appetite with a bag of Lay's salt and vinegar chips. It was 3:00pm already and Lewberg had not gotten back from Schwartzman's. Schwartzman's was a deli up in Pompano which specialized in Montreal style smoked meat sandwiches made famous by the Montreal restaurant whose name they had pretty much ripped off. The NY style pastrami and corned beef which abounded in South Florida could not hold a candle to the smoked meat we had grown up on and the quality at Schwartzman's quite honestly was as close to Schwartz's as was its name.

Anyway, Lewberg had hit his shot on number 15 into the water and thus earned the duty of going on the pick-up.

"Fucking Lewberg went for a drink," muttered Goldfarb. "Keep those chips away from me."

Goldfarb was likely right. Schwartzman's was located in a strip plaza right next to a gentleman's club called The Pleasure Dome. Truth be told, Lewberg wasn't a big fan of those sorts of establishments but the bar stocked Ketel vodka so he put aside whatever philosophical objections he had in favor of a strong drink.

I was about to curse him too but then he walked into the house. I didn't hear him or see him but I could smell the delicious combination of smoked meat, coleslaw, and potato salad.

"About fucking time," said Goldfarb.

"I got some extra karnatzle," said Lewberg. "Plus I emptied their fridge out of cream soda."

"Oh baby!" Exclaimed Goldfarb who had already forgiven Lewberg for his tardiness.

Then Lewberg said "Harold, have you been here all this time?"

And Goldfarb said "Where would I go?"

"Just checking. So I went into the bar to grab a quick Ketel and cran..."

Goldfarb turned to me and said "What did I tell you."

"...and I see this beige Crown Victoria in the VIP parking of the Dome. Right in front of the door."

"Crown Vic eh?" I said. "Nice. Old school. Just like Harold's."

Goldfarb said "The plaza has tons of parking. The guy can't walk twenty feet? Jesus people are so lazy!"

Lewberg said "Nope. VIP, right in front. But here's the thing - the Crown Vic had a personalized license plate."

"What did it say?" I asked.

"Well," replied Lewberg, "see for yourself." He pulled out his phone and laid it out on the table. Then he used two fingers to stretch and expand the photo so we could see it more clearly.

Florida plates.
With a name on them.
And the name was:

Goldfarb

Goldfarb took a big bite of his sandwich and then grabbed a napkin in order to wipe off the excess mustard dribbling down his chin.

He said "Can I see that again?"

Lewberg slid him the phone.

Goldfarb said "Looks exactly like my car."

Lewberg said "I know. Even has your name."

"This is not good," said Goldfarb, shaking his head. "It is December 10th."

I said "What does the date have to do with anything?"

Goldfarb said "My cousin's daughter, Debbie, is getting married on the 20th. Every relative I have, aunts, uncles, nephews, nieces, are coming down to Florida from Canada."

"Is the reception at the Dome?" joshed Lewberg with a smile. "They actually have a great lunchtime buffet."

"Harold," I said, "You are overthinking it."

"I'm not overthinking it. I am thinking it. My entire family goes to Schwartzman's. They are going to see my car with my name in the parking lot of The Pleasure Dome."

"This is South Florida," I argued. "They are going to be eating near the beach."

Goldfarb said "Have you ever been to Torremolinos?"

"Michener put it on the map in The Drifters," offered Lewberg, who always surprised us with his breadth of knowledge. "Tourist town on the Spanish Riviera."

"Yes," agreed Goldfarb. "Huge tourist destination for the English vacationers. And do you know what these English vacationers like to eat when they are in Spain?"

I knew the answer. Even if I didn't know the answer, I knew there was only one place Goldfarb would be going with this.

"Fish and chips. They come all the way from Bristol, from Liverpool, from Manchester, in order to eat in English style pubs and restaurants serving the exact food they had just come from."

"Pompano isn't Torremolinos," I argued. Although I knew it was.

"My family will be going to Schwartzman's at least twice a week."

"Aren't there other Goldfarbs in your family?" Asked Lewberg.

"Nope. Just me. My dad was an only child. All my relatives are from my mother's side. I'm the only Goldfarb. In fact, I'm the only Goldfarb I know."

"Except for the guy in the VIP parking at the Pleasure Dome," I said.

"Maybe he won't be there again," said Lewberg hopefully.

"Yeah, maybe," I said.

But we both knew that was wishful thinking.

The next day, we squeezed into Lewberg's convertible at around 12:30 and headed to Pompano. The three of us had all put on long pants for the occasion. Goldfarb had exchanged his usual slides for a pair of sneakers and one of us, I won't say who, might have even been wearing cologne. We parked across from Schwartzman's and walked to the Pleasure Dome. It was, as Goldfarb had argued, only a few metres away. As we had feared, the beige Crown Victoria was parked in the VIP spot. The doorman, who was marking up a program for the nearby Pompano dog track, asked, without looking up, for $2 for parking. Goldfarb, showing remarkable restraint, pulled out two dollar bills and handed them to the doorman without making an argument about having to pay for free parking.

"Can you tell me who owns that beige Crown Victoria over there?" I asked, pointing to it.

The doorman said "I don't think I remember."

Then Lewberg, in a move so deft it was hard not to assume he had performed it dozens of times before, snatched the bills right out of the doorman's hand and replaced them with a twenty.

"I can't even remember what I had for lunch yesterday," he said with a smile.

"I like this dog in the seventh," said the doorman. "Same name as my first wife, Mildred. She could run like the wind." He circled the name on the program then looked up and said "New owner. Bought the place last month. For another $20 I can tell you his name."

The doorman had a pretty good sense of humor.

The Dome was very dark, very smoky, and was playing very loud music I suspected was also used on Guantanamo Bay prisoners. It

THE BUBBE MEISE AND OTHER STORIES

had a long bar and a buffet set up in the back. There was nobody on the stage and, save for two women I presumed to be dancers sitting at the bar who were busy on their phones and sharing what looked to be a plate of nachos, we were the only people in the entire place. The dancers looked up, I want to say briefly, but it was even shorter than that, when we walked in but then went back to their phones and nachos. In other words, pretty much like any other bar we had ever been in.

The waitress, who already looked like she was counting the hours remaining in her shift, came and took our orders. Goldfarb had his diet coke. Lewberg his Ketel and cran. And I, knowing better than to order a Guinness in a place like this, ordered a Bud Light I knew I would not drink.

When she came back with our orders, Goldfarb asked if we could see the manager.

She said "Hey, I don't make the prices. But I don't blame you, $15 for a freakin' Bud."

Goldfarb said "No, no, the prices are fine. We just wanted to ask him about his car."

"Oh, ok hon."

Two minutes later a man came out. I'm not sure what we were expecting but he was tall and lanky with a full moustache. He was wearing a vest with a huge Lonestar state belt buckle. He looked a little, actually a lot, like the actor Sam Elliot who, amongst other things, played a cowboy in *The Big Lebowski*. Later, in the car ride back, we would all agree he looked like a cowboy. What he did not look like was a Goldfarb.

But, that is who he was. Oscar Goldfarb. Those were the first words out of his mouth when he came to our table and shook our hands.

The second words were "I'll take $50,000 for the car and I'll throw in my Waylon Jennings Greatest Hits CD". Then he winked and said "Truth is, that sonabitch has been stuck in there for two weeks."

Goldfarb said "I'm not so much interested in the car as I am the license plate." He took out his wallet from his pocket and removed his driver's license. "You see," he handed Oscar Goldfarb his license, "my name is Harold Goldfarb."

And Oscar Goldfarb said "No shit. Look at that we are mishpocha," which was maybe the way Jews from Texas pronounced it.

"Yes," answered Goldfarb, "and as mishpocha," Goldfarb delicately pronouncing it, "I wonder if you could do me a favor."

"Anything for a landsman," said Oscar Goldfarb.

"Well," continued Goldfarb, "my family from Canada is coming to Florida next week."

"Canada," exclaimed Oscar Goldfarb. "I heard it was colder than a witch's tit. You couldn't get a pack of wild horses to drag me there."

"Well yes," said Goldfarb tiptoeing through the cliché landmines. "There is a family wedding."

"Mazal tov," said Oscar Goldfarb.

"Thank you," said Goldfarb. "And the family all love to go to Schwartzman's."

"The brisket is to die for," said Oscar Goldfarb.

"It is," said Goldfarb. "The thing is, I also have a beige Crown Victoria and my name is also Goldfarb, and so with your car and its plates parked out front they might get the...."

Oscar Goldfarb held up his hand. "Say no more. You don't need your family thinking that you are spending the day getting, how should I say, getting the wrong type of *naches*. I will park in the back. I could use the walk."

"Thank you, Oscar," said Goldfarb. "I really appreciate it."

"Are you kidding. We Goldfarbs gotta stick together. Let me get you another round of drinks. Maybe you want to meet a couple of the ladies."

"Thanks Oscar," said Goldfarb. "We'll have to take a rain check. Another time. We have a tee time this afternoon."

"Well I envy you. I schlepped my sticks all the way down from Jacksonville and haven't had a chance to play yet. You guys hit them straight. Hell, I'm going to move the car now. Better safe than sorry."

Since we were already here, we decided to have lunch at Schwartzman's. Goldfarb and I had tuna, but Lewberg, who embodied the 'when in Rome' life philosophy, loaded up on smoked meat.

"Well, that was easy," I said.

"Yeah, nice guy," said Lewberg.

"Maybe too easy?" Questioned Goldfarb.

"Sometimes things work out Harold," I said.

"Yeah, maybe you're right," he said, helping himself to half of Lewberg's sandwich. "Hey, you think he was angling for a golf invite?"

"I think he was just being polite," I said.

"Would be a fun guy to play with," Lewberg said, "and the place was empty. He might have a window for 9 holes."

Goldfarb said "Yeah. Wouldn't hurt to ask." He got up and I held up my hand and said "You know what Harold, I'll go, you stay here and pay the bill."

And Goldfarb said "Fair enough. It is the least that I can do."

So I went back to the Dome, paid the doorman another $2 for not parking, allowed my eyes to adjust to the light, and found Oscar Goldfarb behind the main bar. The two dancers were still on their phones. This time they did not even look up.

"Hey partner," he said, "you forget something?"

"We just thought we would invite you to join us for golf this afternoon."

"Well that's mighty kind of you. But I have a contractor coming in this afternoon so I have to stay at my post. Doing some big renovations for the grand re-opening. My turn to take a rain check."

I said "Ok. Anytime."

Lewberg and I didn't really know Goldfarb's cousin Debbie but Goldfarb didn't want to go alone so he scored us an invite to the wedding anyway. It was at the Four Seasons on the beach in Fort Lauderdale and Harold had promised us killer apps and an open bar. Lewberg, in a moment of graciousness, said yes without even asking if they were going to stock Ketel. Goldfarb, looking better than he had in years, was in a tux. In addition to looking good, he was feeling good.

"Five days in a row," he said. "At least one member of my family ate at or picked up food from Schwartzman's five days in a row."

"No sign of the Crown Vic?" I asked.

"Nada. Parked all the way in the back. I checked it out myself."

"Oscar did you a solid," I said.

"Damn straight," replied Goldfarb as he adjusted his tie. "Jesus, I look great! For once a family function which doesn't blow up in my face."

Lewberg and I, though the invitation said black tie, were in sports jackets. Truthfully, we were looking pretty good too. Goldfarb was not lying about the pre-ceremony appetizers. We all basically made a meal of the lollipop lamb chops after positioning ourselves in the exact spot where the wait staff came out of the kitchen. They had set up chairs and the *chuppah* right on the edge of the beach and it really was beautiful. We told Goldfarb we would watch the ceremony from the back row but we slipped out and had a drink at the hotel bar instead. The drinks weren't free but we were spared 45 minutes of aisle marching, endless vows, and readings in Aramaic, Hebrew, and English.

We snuck back in just as the groom stepped on the glass and was greeted with a chorus of *l'chayims*.

It was also at the exact same time the small prop plane, dragging an advertising banner, like the type which routinely dotted the skies above the beach, appeared above our heads.

Everyone looked up at the same time. I had to admit, it was a catchy banner.

"Goldfarb's Strip Club: Let our talented dancers show you what mazel really is."

THE HOODIE

Photograph courtesy artistshot.com

It is the Aria on a Saturday night. My friends and I had been hiking in Zion National Park in Utah and were now in Vegas for two days of chill before heading back to Toronto. But their idea of chill was Barry Manilow's early show at the Mirage.

I wasn't going to do that.

There is some back and forth, but I am not going to budge. We agree to meet later for dinner.

I now have two hours to kill.

I wander over to the poker room. It is packed. Am looking for a low-stakes game where I can kill a few hours and not lose my shirt. But the lists for those games are huge.

"I can get you on the $5–$10 no-limit," says the hostess.

I shake my head no. Those are much higher stakes than I am used to. Also, the people who play in those games are generally pros or semi-pros. They aren't tourists from Akron, Ohio. Or, in my case, from Toronto, Canada.

The players in those games just can't wait for guys like me.

So I take a lap around the casino. It takes me 10 minutes. I look at my phone. I now still have an hour and 48 minutes to kill.

I could leave the Aria and find a lower-stake game at another casino. But that seems like a lot of work. I am a pretty good poker player. I can probably play with these guys. They put their pants on one proverbial leg at a time like I do. Even the women.

I go back to the hostess.

"That seat on $5–$10 still open?"

"Yes, hon. Go buy chips at the cashier."

I go to the cashier and ask what the minimum buy-in is for the $5–$10 game. The cashier tells me it is $500 but nobody buys in for only $500.

I say, "Let me have $500 please."

I sit at the table and unpack my chips from the chip rack.

It doesn't take long.

The other players at the table have stacks of chips which look like rows of high-rise apartments. My chips look like a pup tent pitched in the backyard.

I have barely had time to sit down when I get dealt my first hand. It is a pretty good starting hand. A King and a Queen. A kid in a baseball cap next to me raises to $50. Jesus, this is a big game. I call. Everyone else folds. The baseball cap smiles at me.

The flop comes King, five, four. There are two hearts.

I have a pair of Kings. But I am worried about the flush. I bet $100. Am hoping it is enough to get him to fold.

But it's not.

He calls.

The fourth card is not a heart. It is a harmless two of clubs. I don't have much choice. I go all in. It is the right play. Now I know why $500 is not enough to start with.

My heart is pounding. I have played a lot of poker. Thousands and thousands of hands. But my heart is pounding.

I am hoping he is going to fold and I am going to win the very first hand I played. I might even pack up my chips and call it a night with a nice little win. Look what I did while you guys were listening to Mandy.

But he calls.

Shows the Q8 of hearts.

I feel sick. How can he call here? It isn't even the best flush draw.

I look up to see if he will flash a sheepish grin. Sorry, I know I wasn't getting the odds but I just felt it kind of look.

But no.

He looks like he is thrilled to turn over his Q8 of hearts.

Of course he gets the two of hearts on the river and I have lost the entire $500 in the first hand. I reach into my pocket and pull out $500 more. I can't leave after only one hand.

I look around the table to see if I can solicit an ounce of sympathy. A wry shake of the head which really means 'what an idiot.' Or a terse smile which says 'no worries—you played it right.'

But no. Nothing. Everyone is on their phones and have moved to the next hand.

It is the Aria on a Saturday night and I am not the first person to have a flush run him down. A woman orders a drink from the buxom waitress and then gets up and leaves the table. When the waitress returns with her vodka martini straight up with a twist, the woman, who looked to be in her early 20s, with $10,000 in chips in front of her, is still not back. The drink is free but a tip is obligatory. I look around the table. She has been chatting amicably with a bunch of the others. But no one makes a move. I toss a $5 chip and barely get a nod of thanks.

The woman comes back. The drink is now in front of her. Will anyone at the table tell her I was the one who tipped the waitress? Apparently not. I keep my mouth shut. We are playing for thousands of dollars and I am not going to be the dick who pipes up for a measly five bucks. But it gnaws at me. So when she splashes the pot a few hands later with a big raise, I decide to defend my blind with the 9,10 of clubs.

The flop comes three hearts, I check and she comes out betting. I don't have a heart. I have absolutely nothing. It is an easy fold.

But now I have a bug up my ass about the fucking tip which I didn't get thanked for.

So, instead of folding, I declare all in. I'm going to make the big bluff and just steal the hand from her. Old school. She shrugs her shoulders, announces call, and turns over two hearts. She has the flush. All I have is egg on my face.

So now I'm reaching for my third buy-in, feeling especially sick, because the only thing worse than being a dick is being a tourist who looks like he has watched too much poker on TV.

I was now in for $1500.

I keep my head down, because I don't want to see them trading knowing glances about what a complete piece-of-shit poker player I am.

I vow to play super tight and only consider premium hands.

I fold and fold and fold.

So when two red Aces fall into my hand in early position, I decide to play a little tricky and I just call, hoping someone will raise and I can re-raise.

But there is no raise.

I have been at the table for over an hour and can't recall a single hand which wasn't raised. It is a super aggressive table.

But now I get Aces and it's call call call call call. What the fuck? And six people are in the hand.

So now I know I am about to bust. I know the Aces are about to get cracked. I just don't know how.

But I don't have to wait long.

A 2,4,6 rainbow flop, three different suits. My nemesis in the baseball cap bets $75 and gets rid of everyone before it comes back to me. There is enough money in the pot and I don't want to see another card so I announce all in. The words are barely out of my mouth when the baseball cap calls, shoving his chips into the pot with one hand and turning over the 3,5 unsuited with the other.

He has flopped the straight.

He doesn't owe me an excuse, but he shrugs his shoulders and announces anyway, "Dude, you didn't raise those pocket rockets before the flop."

The two miracle cards don't come and I am out.

I stagger from the table. I am shellshocked. I have taken 10 steps when I remember I have left my *Muskoka Life is Good* sweatshirt draped over the chair. But there is no way I am going back for it. I think I hear someone call out. But they don't know my name. And anyway, am not going back.

I splash some water in my face in the washroom and the guy next to me is doing the same.

I can sense he wants to tell me his bad beat. Some crazy only-one-card-in-the-deck kind of story. But I have heard them all. I have lived them all.

I step back out to the casino and the cold air conditioning gives me a chill.

I meet my friends in front of the designated restaurant. They said the show was amazing. What did I do all this time, they ask.

"Not much," I say. "I just walked around. Oh"—I hold up my new Aria Casino hoodie—"and I bought a new hoodie."

"Nice," one friend says. "How much was it?"

And I say, "Don't ask."

I'M NOT GOLDFARB

Photograph © David Reed / pixabay.com

Lewberg called and said he was taking the dog to the park. I should come with him. I told him I couldn't think of anything I wanted to do less than walk his dog in the park. He said the park was full of women walking their dogs. He said it was a beautiful day. He said his dog missed me. He said a plastic cup of Ketel and cranberry wouldn't kill anyone.

I said okay.

It was a beautiful day.

We weren't in the park for more than five minutes when we ran into Sandy Abramson walking her cockapoo.

Sandy Abramson was a woman I used to date. It was one of those Halley's Comet types of relationships where the breakup was truly and honestly mutual. I didn't see her that often but when I did, I didn't have to duck behind a tree. It's not like she was Heather Lewis.

I don't really like running into ex-girlfriends, but I was genuinely pleased to see Sandy Abramson.

She, on the other hand, was not happy to see me.

She looked pissed.

I said hi.

Lewberg said hi.

Sandy Abramson said, "We dated for two years."

It was a weird greeting but I had no idea where she was going with it so I just said, "Yeah."

"We lived together for a year."

I said, "Yeah."

"Two years and I don't get a single mention in your book?"

Now if anyone else had said that I would have laughed because it was such a hilarious deadpan bit. It was really classic. But Sandy Abramson wasn't really known for her sense of humor. It was one of the reasons we broke up.

I didn't really know what to say. I mean, I don't think I really had any good Sandy Abramson stories.

It was one of the reasons we broke up.

"I mean it is so fucking passive aggressive. So fucking typical."

So I say, "Sandy, the book sold 14 copies. Lewberg bought 10. Nobody cares."

I couldn't understand why Sandy Abramson would give a shit.

"Look," she said, "I don't care. I just think it's weird. What about that time in Florida?"

I had no idea about any time in Florida. But then I decided to do what I do best.

I lied.

"Well if you must know, you're Amanda."

Lewberg took a very big gulp of his vodka cranberry. He then turned his back on us.

"Amanda?"

"Harold Goldfarb's ex-girlfriend. In Get Your Affairs in Order."

In for a penny, in for a pound.

"The suicide story?"

"Exactly."

" I don't watch the Cooking Channel."

"Well, I had to disguise it. Remember how much you loved those National Geographic documentaries?"

We had never seen a National Geographic documentary. But Sandy Abramson seemed placated.

"Oh, Amanda. Yeah. I see that. Sorry for being such a dick. I just thought it was a bit weird. Amanda. Okay."

And then I said, "As if I would ever leave you out."

Then Sandy Abramson said, "Wait, if I am Amanda, does that make you Goldfarb?"

So I say, "No, I am me. Goldfarb is a fictional character. But I needed an ex-girlfriend and so..."

Sandy Abramson said, "Got it."

We hugged and then Sandy Abramson and her cockapoo went on their way.

Lewberg, who had an empty plastic cup in one hand and a plastic bag of dog shit in the other, turned to me and said:

"Sandy Abramson is not Amanda."

And I said, "No, she's not."

Then Lewberg said, "This is not going to end well."

I said, "What are you talking about? I just made her day. That's what I do. I please people."

Lewberg said, "Do you see this bag of shit? If I had to choose between being you right now or this bag of shit, I would choose this bag of shit 10 times out of 10."

Lewberg was dead wrong.

For about eight hours.

My phone rings and it is the wife of a friend of mine. Am going to call her Debbie. She is one of those really, really nice people. Like for no reason at all. Just to be nice. I sometimes feel bad questioning her sincerity because I really feel she is being genuine. I just don't understand people like that.

I say, "Hey."

She says hey back but she stretches it out to last about 10 seconds. At first it sounds like a 'I am having a surprise Zoom birthday party for my husband' hey and 'could you make one of your funny videos.'

But it's not.

"How are you doing?" she wants to know. Now I recognize it. It is the 'how are you doing' the week after my mother died. Then the month after my mother died. Then six months after my mother died. I kinda thought it was nice: I'm lucky if I can remember to call once.

"All is good." I said. "Things are great."

"Oh, that's good. That is so good. You have to keep your spirits up."

My spirits had been fine. Now they were starting to sink.

Instead I said, "Thanks for checking in. I really appreciate it."

She said, "Call whenever you want to talk. Day or night."

And I said, "Okay. Thanks."

She said, "So many people love you."

"Thanks, Debbie, I really appreciate it." I did. But wasn't happy about why she was concerned.

I heard call waiting. I said, "Debbie, I have to go."

Then I spoke to a very nice man about getting my eavestroughs cleaned. We spoke for about 20 minutes. I didn't have the heart to tell him I lived in a condo.

Then I called Lewberg.

He picked up on the first ring.

I said, "We have a situation."

Lewberg, the good friend he is, did not correct me by saying I was the one who had a situation. He did however say, "That's why I picked the bag of shit."

I ignored him.

"I just got off the phone with Debbie Marchment."

"She still asking you about your dead mother?"

"She is nice," I said. "You could learn a little from her."

"I made a very nice donation," said Lewberg.

"She is very concerned about my wellbeing. She told me that people loved me."

"That is crazy," said Lewberg. "Nobody loves you."

I ignored him.

"Do you know who Debbie Marchment's best friend is?" I asked. But it was a rhetorical question. Of course Lewberg knew.

Debbie Marchment's best friend was Sandy Abramson.

Sandy Abramson thought she was Amanda.

Sandy Abramson thought I was Goldfarb.

Now Debbie Marchment thought I was Goldfarb.

Oh to be a bag of shit right now.

Then Lewberg spoke and lifted my spirits ever so slightly.

He said what he always said:

"I think I have a guy."

"This is a really dumb idea," I said to Lewberg's guy, who was eating his smoked meat sandwich like a man on death row eating his final meal. Lewberg and I had finished our sandwiches 15 minutes ago.

Lewberg's guy dipped a french fry into a mound of ketchup and rotated it for 20 seconds so every part of the fry was covered in ketchup before popping it into his mouth.

"Don't look at me," he said as he carefully contemplated another fry. "I think it is a bad idea too."

Lewberg, who had already finished his fries, helped himself to a ketchup-less handful, took a gulp of his cream soda—okay, Ketel and cream soda—and said:

"It isn't a dumb idea. It is a brilliant idea. Jimmie here," he pointed to his guy, "goes into the park with his cockapoo. These cockapoo owners are drawn to each other like flies to fucking honey. He strikes up a conversation with Sandy Abramson. *How do you do, how do you do. My name is Harold Goldfarb. Really? You are Harold Goldfarb? Yes, I am Harold Goldfarb.* And there you go. Bob's your uncle."

"Bob's your uncle?" I say.

Lewberg says, "Yeah. Easy as pie. Now you are no longer Goldfarb." He pointed to his guy, who had motioned the waitress and ordered another sandwich and plate of fries. "He is."

I said, "This might be the dumbest idea I have ever heard." I turned to Lewberg's guy and said, "What do you think?"

Lewberg's guy said, "I also think it is the dumbest idea I have ever heard, but for $500 a day plus expenses, I can be Harold Goldfarb or Ho Chi Minh. It's your money."

"What expenses?" I asked.

"Well, a snack for me and the dog."

I turned to Lewberg. "You can get us a cockapoo?"

"Yes," he said. "I've got a guy."

"This will never work," I said.

"That's because you're not a dog guy. These cockapoo owners become best friends. They are like family. They tell each other everything." Then he too ordered another plate of fries and poured a little more Ketel into his glass of cream soda.

Seven absolutely beautiful dog-walking days in a row and seven days when there was absolutely no sign of Sandy Abramson.

I didn't know where she was walking her fucking cockapoo, but it wasn't in the park.

Meanwhile, I was paying Lewberg's guy $500 a day to walk the cockapoo and Lewberg's other guy $250 a day to rent the cockapoo.

It was a fucking nightmare!

In the meantime, Debbie Marchment had gathered a team of friends and acquaintances who were calling me every day to check up on me. They were taking shifts.

I wasn't suicidal. I might have been a little homicidal.

I was about to call the whole thing off, but then on day eight, Sandy Abramson and her cockapoo showed up at the park.

Lewberg and I hid behind the public restrooms on the far side of the park.

I had to hand it to Lewberg. He knew his cockapoo owners. Sandy Abramson made a beeline for Lewberg's guy who was walking Lewberg's other guy's rented cockapoo.

They had an animated conversation for about five minutes and Sandy Abramson hugged Lewberg's guy.

It was not a short hug.

Next thing I knew, Lewberg's guy was walking towards us, handed the rented cockapoo to Lewberg, and half-jogged into the restroom declaring he had to whiz like a proverbial race horse. When he came out, wiping his hands on his trousers, he pointed to Lewberg and announced, "This man is a genius."

"It went well?" I asked.

"Worked like a charm," he said. "She said she felt so stupid thinking you were Goldfarb when you couldn't possibly be Goldfarb. Because I was Goldfarb." Lewberg's guy grabbed Lewberg's Ketel and cranberry and took a triumphant swig.

"She really said that?" I could not believe this idiotic plan had worked.

"Yup," said Lewberg's guy. "She bought it hook, line and motherfucking sinker. I laid it on thick. Told her I couldn't believe you had betrayed my trust. That I had told you that story in confidence."

"Betrayed your trust?" I looked at Lewberg but he was all of a sudden very interested in his shoelaces.

"Nobody said anything about betraying trust. Lewberg, did anyone say anything about betraying anyone's trust?"

Lewberg ignored me.

I turned to Lewberg's guy. "We never said anything about betraying anyone's trust," I whispered.

Lewberg's guy shrugged his shoulders and said, "A little improv. No extra charge. Can I have that $4000 now?"

So just like that, I had turned from being a perfectly nice fellow who had written a book to a perfectly fine fellow with suicidal thoughts who had written a book to a complete asshole who had betrayed a friend's confidence just so he could write a book.

Debbie Marchment stopped calling. Most of my friends stopped calling. Lewberg still called. He envied me. He kept asking for tips on how he could lose all his friends. "Tell me who to betray and I would do it in a second," he said.

"I didn't betray anyone," I argued stupidly.

"Just remind me not to tell you anything in confidence," joked Lewberg. "Poor Goldfarb. The humiliation."

The eavestrough guy kept calling though, and I finally hired him to clean the eavestroughs of my brother's house. He did a pretty good job.

But then he stopped calling too.

Finally I called Lewberg's other guy and bought myself a cockapoo.

Every day I get in the car and we drive to a park clear on the other side of town. Where I don't know anyone. We go on long walks. There's a lady who walks her scotch terrier who I have seen a few times. Today I give her a halfhearted wave and she waves back and drags her reluctant terrier to the bench where I have stopped to drink water and give my dog a snack.

 "Cockapoo?"'she asks.

"Yes," I say. " Cockapoo."

"What's his name?"

"Oh," I reply reaching down to pick up the dog so she can have a better look.

"His name? His name is Goldfarb."

THE STINGRAY STORY

Photograph © Roger Darnell / pixabay.com

I have some people over for drinks in my backyard. There is Allie, Cory, Lewberg, Candace, and Candace's new boyfriend whose name I don't catch. I have learned—by the look on the faces of my guests maybe not learned well enough—how to make whiskey sours, and we are social distancing and talking about antibodies and immunity.

Not really my favorite topic, but I'm okay with it because it is a nice night, the whiskey sours start tasting a little bit better after your second, and it gives me a chance to tell my stingray story.

So I wait for a little gap in the conversation, somewhere between COVID, Spanish flu, mumps and measles, and jump in with my, "Have I ever told you my stingray story?"

As it happens, only Allie has heard the stingray story, and, to her credit, or likely as a result of one too many whiskey sours, instead of saying, "Nobody wants to hear your stingray story," says, "That is a good story."

Every once in a while, you are reminded why you are friends with someone and this is one of those times.

I top off everyone's drinks and then announce this might be a good time to go pee.

Then Allie, who maybe isn't quite as drunk as I might have thought, says, "Why don't you tell the short version?"

Nobody makes a move to the bathroom. I think that's on them. It's their bladders.

In the spring of 1975, I took a week-long school-sanctioned field trip with five classmates to the Malaysian island of Tioman.

I had been going to school in Singapore at the United World College of Southeast Asia. This, for reasons I still have yet to comprehend, was part of the curriculum: a one-week camping trip.

So six of us took two taxis to the Malaysian border. Three Germans.
An Australian.
A Zoroastrian Indian.

And a Canadian Jew.

One of us was lugging a 25 hp outboard motor.

I can tell you it wasn't the Canadian Jew.

We then hitchhiked up the Malaysian coast to the fishing village of Mersing.

Allie, who now seems a little drunker, says, "There is no way your parents let you hitchhike up the Malaysian coast."

I cast her a glance. I don't like the flow of my story interrupted. "With a 25 hp outboard engine," she adds, now giggling.

But she is right—the notion of my parents letting me go camping for a week on a remote island with five sixteen-year-old classmates and hitchhiking there to boot sounds, well, to borrow from Wallace Shawn, inconceivable.

I might have mentioned we were going to be accompanied by a faculty advisor.

The distance between Singapore and Mersing is 120 km. I looked it up. It takes us 10 hours to get there. Turns out, not too many people want to stop and pick up six students and a 25 hp motor. Finally, a trucker takes pity on us. We sprawl out on the lumber on his flatbed.

The last ferry has left hours ago. But, I soon learn, we were never going to take the ferry. The ferry was only for guests of the newly built resort on the other side of the island. We weren't staying at the resort. I ask if there is a campsite. The Australian says not so much a campsite as a deserted beach.

Okay then.

We pool our resources and hire a Malay fisherman to shuttle us the 50 km across the Mersing straight to Tioman Island. It is a two-hour ride. There is much drinking. By the three Germans, the Australian, and the Zoroastrian Indian. The Canadian Jew does not drink. He spends a lot of time worrying about sharks and falling off the boat.

We get deposited 50 metres from the beach and wade in in the dark. It could be Haifa 1947. I carry the outboard motor. Everyone else is too drunk. We all pass out on the beach.

They say youth is wasted on the young, but when we woke up the next day, each of us, all only 16 years old, five of us very hungover, one of us wondering where the hell you were supposed to take a shit, all of us, to a man, understood we were in paradise. The sky was bluer than we had ever seen. That water was clearer than we had ever seen or would ever see. The reef below could be explored without snorkels or goggles. The beach went on forever. One of the

Germans climbed a tree and we breakfasted on fresh coconut and ramen noodles. The coconuts cut in half by a machete which was in a rowboat along with fishing rods and nets which had magically washed up on our beach while we were sleeping. I guess arrangements had been made.

The plan was to take the nets and harvest smaller fish to be used as bait for a night fishing expedition.

"Night fishing?" says Allie. "You were going night fishing? This part is definitely made up. You wouldn't even go day fishing."

She is beginning to get on my nerves.

"Look," I say, "Whose story is this?"

"When are we getting to the part about the stingray?" says Lewberg, emboldened by Allie's constant interruptions. "This part is getting a little bit boring."

"I'm just getting to it. It's coming right up. Jesus, give a man a chance."

So I am in the shallow water. Water barely higher than my knee. With a net in my hand when I feel a really, really sharp sting on my ankle.

I drop the net and crash into the shallow water and see the stingray, which had been minding its own business until I stepped on it, float off.

My cries for help are ignored.
To be fair, only moments before I had put on a pretty convincing shark attack pantomime. Eventually, one of the Germans wanders over and drags me onto the beach.
The pain is intense.
I am on my back and they have balled up a towel and elevated my foot.

The island caretaker suddenly appears on a moped. He is a large man and the moped sags from his weight. If I weren't writhing in pain, I would have laughed. He says something but we can't make it out because he is so soft-spoken. We ask him to repeat it. He does. Nobody has a clue what he is saying. We say, please, one more time. So he gets off the moped and kneels right next to me on the beach. He leans over. It smells like he had coconut and ramen noodles for breakfast too. This time I hear what he says.

He says, "You shouldn't elevate the leg. It allows the poison to run to the heart." I say nothing, but in my head I'm thinking, 'Are you fucking kidding me?'
The caretaker continues, "Someone should suck the venom out."
Someone.

Not him. Someone.

One of the Germans, in a moment of minor heroism, leans over and proceeds to, as best as he can, suck the venom out of the small cut in my ankle.

My story is then interrupted by Candace's new boyfriend. It is the first time we meet him. There was a little discussion about whether he should have been invited at all. Anyway, he has not said a word all night. And now he is interrupting my story. He too, like the caretaker, is soft-spoken. But I hear what he says. And I immediately take a shine to him. Later that night I will call Candace and tell her I really like her new boyfriend.

What he says is, "Doctor said you are going to die."

It is a punchline to a joke.

Anyway, I'm not sure anyone heard or understood him. But I appreciated it.

The venom does not go to my heart. The pain is excruciating, but the Australian, for reasons that are not at all clear, seems to have some codeine.

My ankle gets bandaged. I manage to hop around for a week. I don't go back into the water.

The caretaker sees us off on the last day. He has arranged for us to go back to Mersing on the official ferry. Turns out getting stung by a stingray on Tioman earns you some island cred.

He asks me how I am.
I say good.
I don't mention the codeine.
I say, "The stingray barely nicked me. Why did it hurt so much? The cut was not deep at all." He says, "The pain comes from the venom. The stingray venom is one of the most painful."
I give him a wide grin and say, "I know."
He says, "The good news is you now have lifetime immunity from stingray venom."
Allie says, "Oh, yeah, now I remember why this story is about immunity."
I say, "You are ruining it."
She says, "No, I'm not. They don't know where this is going."
The new boyfriend now speaks for the second time.
"You stepped on another stingray?" he asks a bit sheepishly.
I glare at Allie. "I am going to fucking kill you," I say, but I am smiling.
"You really stepped on another stingray?" asks Candace.
"Yes," I concede, realizing the story is now shot. "10 years later in Israel. In Eilat."
"No immunity?"
"Nope. Hurt like a bitch."
Everyone is silent for a few seconds.
Then someone pipes up.

"It's still a good story."
Everyone agrees it is still a good story.
I glare at Allie.
"Good story," she says with a smile. "It's one of my favorites."

STRAIGHT SETS

Photograph © seoterra / 123rf.com

My Uncle Henri would not stop going on about Peter Raymond.

"Did you call Peter Raymond? Did you make an appointment with Peter Raymond? Why don't I see anything in your report about Peter Raymond?"

He had a bug up his ass about Peter Raymond.

Peter Raymond was the senior purchasing agent for Jackson Exhaust. Jackson Exhaust was a huge automotive parts manufacturer which used a clear powder coating to paint their exhausts. We made clear powder coatings. But Jackson Exhaust did not buy their clear powder coating from us. They bought it from Samson Paint—our biggest competitor.

My Uncle Henri did not understand why Jackson Exhaust did not buy clear powder coating from us.

"We have a beautiful clear," he said. If you closed your eyes, you would think you were listening to the late Egyptian President Anwar Sadat. If Sadat was the owner of a powder coating company and not the President of Egypt.

He was right of course.

We did make a beautiful clear powder coating.

But ours was not on the Jackson Exhaust automotive approval list.

Also, ours was about $1.00/kg more expensive.

Peter Raymond told me as much whenever he deemed to pick up the phone when I called him. He told me I was wasting my time. He told me they were very happy with Samson Paint.

But when I told my Uncle Henri these things, he looked at me as if I had just told him Yvan Cournoyer was not a fast skater. As if I had just told him his wife, my Tante Nandi, did not know how to cook.

"Ronnie," he lectured. "How many times have I told you. When they throw you out the front door, you sneak back in through the window."

I loved my Uncle Henri. But there is no way he ever snuck in through a window.

"I am coming to Toronto next week. I want you to make an appointment with Peter Raymond."

Peter Raymond would not take my calls. He would not return my messages. So I drove to Jackson Automotive and told reception I was here to see Peter Raymond. Did I have an appointment? I did not. "You should make an appointment." I tried to make an appointment. He won't return my calls. "You should make an appointment." I said, "Can you just tell him Ron Zevy of Protech Chemicals is here? I just need two minutes. I am happy to wait."

So I waited.

Six hours.

Three times Peter Raymond walked right by me, twice I presume on the way to the bathroom, and once on the way to an extended lunch with Mario Rossetti of Samson Paint.

Not once did he acknowledge my existence.

The receptionist smiled at me a few times. But I don't think she felt sorry for me. Nobody ever told me to go into powder paint sales.

Peter Raymond left his office door slightly ajar. I tilted my head just so I could see he was playing solitaire on his computer.

Red Queen on black King, you fucking piece of shit.

Finally at 4:55, the receptionist picked up her ringing phone and motioned me in.

I got straight to the point.

"My boss (I didn't say my Uncle) is coming into town. He wants five minutes to say hello. He knows you are happy with Samson Paint. He just wants to say hi."

"Sounds like a waste of five minutes," said Peter Raymond. I was going to tell him it was my job on the line but he agreed before I had to prostrate myself. But first he put the black 9 on the red 10.

Jesus, what an asshole.

Our appointment was at 10:00 am. Peter Raymond let us in at 11:55. My Uncle, God bless him, went to the bathroom three times while we waited.

"Your salesman here is quite persistent," said Peter Raymond.

My Uncle had a whole pitch ready for Peter Raymond. Five times he had repeated it to me in the car. How we had a better product. How we would provide better service. How cheap was going to cost them money in the long run. It was good. But I knew it wasn't going to work. But when we got into Peter Raymond's office, my Uncle Henri decided to call an audible.

This is what he said to Peter Raymond:

"You play tennis?"

I had no idea where he had come up with this, but then I saw the Donnay racquet, the one Björn Borg played with, propped up in the corner of the office. My Uncle had gone all Kevin Spacey in *The Usual Suspects* on us. He did that. He looked at family pictures. He looked at paintings on the wall. He looked for tennis racquets.

Peter Raymond reached over, grabbed the racquet and twirled it in his hand. He looked more like a majorette than a tennis player.

"Only in the summer," he said. "Too damn expensive to play indoors in the winter."

My Uncle Henri replied, "I know it is expensive." He pointed at me. "This one expenses it. I pay for it!"

He was right, I expensed my membership to Mayfair Country Club which had indoor courts.

Then my Uncle Henri threw me under the bus.

"I'm sure Ronnie would be happy to bring you to his club."

Then he shook Peter Raymond's hand and said goodbye.

Not a word about powder coatings.

Not a word.

When we got in the car, Uncle Henri decided to back up the bus and run me over a few more times.

"Are you a good tennis player?" He asked.

I said I was pretty good.

"Well," he said as he buckled up, "you have to let him win."

So for three months, every Wednesday night, I played tennis with Peter Raymond. Peter Raymond was shit. Every Wednesday, he beat me in straight sets. I would hit the ball long. I would hit the ball into the net. I would double fault. Peter Raymond beat me in straight sets every Wednesday. Then we would have a beer, to be fair, he had three, and he would give me tennis tips. I needed to bend my knees. I wasn't tossing the ball high enough.

I would write it into my report.

Played tennis with Peter Raymond.

Lost 6-3, 6-4.

My uncle was making another sales trip to Toronto. Could I set up another meeting with Peter Raymond? Peter Raymond said yes without batting an eye. Meeting was set for 10:00 am. He met us at 10:00 am.

"Henri, you've got yourself quite the salesman here," said Peter Raymond. "But maybe you should let him expense a few tennis lessons. I try giving him tips but he is really bad. And not getting better. He hasn't won a single set."

But my Uncle Henri did not want to talk about tennis. He wanted to talk about clear powder coating.

"Peter," he said slowly and carefully. "We would like a chance. Let us show you what we can do."

And then Peter Raymond shocked the hell out of me by saying, "Let's do a 10,000 kgs trial."

My Uncle Henri said, "Great."

Peter Raymond said, "Henri, these things take time. It isn't overnight."

Uncle Henri said, "We aren't in a rush. We are interested in a long-term relationship."

Peter Raymond said, "We know your paint. We have heard good things. It just has to pass the roof test."

I said, "Roof test?"

"Yes, we coat about 15 exhausts and put them on our roof for six months. We see how it deals with the sun and the elements."

Six months, I thought. Six months was a piece of cake. Our polyester clear could withstand six months in the sun standing on its head. Six months was nothing. I couldn't believe we were going to get the Jackson Exhaust account.

We all shook hands. Peter reconfirmed our Wednesday tennis match.

I knew better than to wait for praise from my Uncle, but I still fished for a compliment.

"10,000 kgs is a nice order," I said. "Sounds like they are serious."

My Uncle didn't say anything. I knew a compliment was a long shot. I didn't care. It was a nice order.

"I'll call the lab and tell them to send a sample for the roof test. Our polyester clear will have no problem passing. Six months is easy."

Then my Uncle said something which really surprised me:

"Don't bother."

I didn't understand. And I said so.

"We don't want to do business with these guys."

"Uncle Henri," I argued. "You have been bugging me about Jackson Exhaust for years. I have been playing tennis with Peter Raymond for three months and letting him win. We finally get an order and now you don't want to do business with them? I really don't understand."

My Uncle Henri turned to me. "You know anything about car exhausts?" It had to be a rhetorical question because he knew I didn't know anything about car exhausts. I told him no.

"When the car starts, it generates so much heat that the paint gets burned off the very first time."

I told him I didn't know that. "What do they need the paint for then?"

"It's just for display purposes. So it looks shiny and nice for the customer. When you go into," he struggled to remember the name of the car part store but then remembered, "like Napa Auto Parts."

I said I didn't understand. "Why would they want to test sun resistance by putting it on the roof for six months if it never gets exposed to the sun?"

"Because," he said as he popped one of my Tante Nandi's sambouseks into his mouth. "They are idiots."

"I agree. Peter Raymond is an idiot. But it is a pretty good order."

He wagged his finger at me.

"If there is one guy doing something dumb it means there is another guy letting him do something dumb. Who knows how many dumb people they have running the company."

I said, "Okay."

"Don't worry," he said. "There are other companies." Then he said something even more surprising than turning down a big order. "You didn't do a bad job."

I said thanks.

Then he said, "But it took you three years." But he was smiling when he said it.

Jackson Exhaust went out of business two years later. We heard they owed Samson Paint a lot of money. That's what we heard.

I only played tennis with Peter Raymond one more time.

I beat him in straight sets.

6-0, 6-0.

I guess his tennis tips paid off.

GETTING A HAIRCUT

My friend David Matlow is pissed off he is not in any of my stories. He doesn't understand why I don't tell the chair story. I tell him his version of the chair story and my version of the chair story are not the same.

David and his wife Leanne insist I once asked to borrow chairs from them for a party I did not invite them to.

Which never happened.

I say, "If I tell the chair story, I would probably have to start the story by saying my friend David Matlow is a big fat liar." He says he is okay with that.

Although he doesn't think he is fat.

I say, "No, I really don't want to tell the chair story."

"I'll tell you what—I can, if he wants, give him a mention in my haircut in Israel story."

"A mention?"

"Yes," I say, "I can mention it in passing. Like, speaking of haircuts in Israel, my friend David Matlow, who lives in Toronto, only ever gets his hair cut in Israel. That kind of thing."

"A mention."

David is a bit bitter. He says, "Harold Rosen got an entire"—the time I took him to buy a mattress—"story devoted to him."

I tell him, "I understand, but a mention in passing is the best I can do."

"Any chance you can say I own the largest Theodor Herzl memorabilia collection in the world?"

I say, "Absolutely not."

He thinks about it and says, "Okay, do you want the name of my Israeli barber?"

I say, "Tell you what—let me circle back with you."

This is the story about getting my haircut in Israel.

I was in Israel for a wedding. My sister said, "Your hair is a mess. Go to Natan and get a haircut." Natan is her son and my nephew. He is a barber and has set up shop in a small space on the ground floor of his building. I gave him a call. He was thrilled to hear from me. I told him, "I am coming for a haircut." He said, "*Achi* (Hebrew slang for 'my brother'), I am slammed here. They are lined up out the door. Give me two hours." I said, "I will be there in five minutes."

Am going to be honest now. The only reason I am writing this story is so I can tell my favourite Natan story. I couldn't figure out where to fit it in, so I am sticking it right here.

I should begin by saying Natan is one of the most charming people you could ever hope to meet. In a movie, he would be the lovable con man. Actually, in life he is the lovable con man.

Natan calls me up one day and says:

"Uncle Ronnie, I have a proposition."

So now I know this is going to cost me money. I just don't know how much yet.

"Okay, Natan," I say. "Go ahead. I'm listening."

He says, "I want to buy a new car."

I say that sounds nice.

He says yeah. "I'll pay for half and you'll pay for half."

I say that sounds good. "Where are you going to get your half?"

And he says—I love this part—"That is what I wanted to talk to you about."

Natan wasn't lying. His shop was full of ultra-Orthodox boys, and some of their mothers, waiting to get their haircuts. He had the music blaring and he was moving in between two chairs. Cutting hair back and forth. He was like Bobby Fischer at an exhibition chess match.

He gave me a big hug.

"Uncle Ronnie," he said, surveying my hair, "you came just in time."

I said, "Okay, *yallah*, let's start. I still have to drive to Jerusalem."

He said, "You can't wait?"

I said no. It had to be now.

He said, "*Beseder habibi*," and walked over and turned off the boombox.

The room went silent and he made an announcement:

"My uncle Ronnie from America is giving everyone 100 shekels ($20) to buy candy for Purim."

He turned to me and gave me a thumbs-up.

The crowd lined up to get their cash. Am pretty sure some people came in from the street.

Then he gave me a fantastic $500 haircut.

I realize I forgot to give David his mention. I got all caught up in the whole $500 haircut thing that it completely slipped my mind. I feel bad about it and put off calling him for a couple of days.

He takes it pretty well.

I tell him I am sorry. I feel really bad about it. He says, "No worries, all good." The phone is silent for a few seconds. "It was the $500 haircut story?" he asks. I say yeah. "Good story," he says. I say yeah. "Did you get in the Natan car loan story? I love that story." I say, "Yeah. It was a bit of a stretch but I managed to squeeze it in." He says, "That's good. It is a great story." I say, "Yeah. Listen, I will try to get you in the next one." He says, "No worries, Ron. I did tell a couple of people, but it's all good." I say, "Okay. I appreciate you being understanding." He says, "No problem. That is what friends do." I say, "Speaking of friends, I have a bunch coming over for dinner. Could I maybe borrow a couple of chairs?"

RONNIE 2.0

Photograph © Jose Losada / Unsplash

Pretty much everyone I knew told me it was time to upgrade my operating system. I ignored them. The default system I was born with had served me very well all of these years. I wasn't about to change because of a bunch of disgruntled, complaining naysayers. Then Rena, my niece, pulled me aside and told me it was time. Nothing pains her more than hurting another human being, so I knew if she was telling me, it had to be true.

So I called the 1-800 number that night. I didn't have to look it up because I passed their giant billboard on the highway every night when I drove home from work.

The recorded message said due to a heavy call volume, the wait time might be 10 to 15 minutes. I almost hung up, but that is exactly what my old operating system would have done, so I held on. My patience was rewarded because the hold music was one of my all-time favorite songs—Dancing in the Moonlight. So I was pretty pissed off when Keith answered after two minutes.

"This is Keith. How can I help you?"

"The message said 10 to 15 minutes. I didn't even get to hear the end of the song."

"We aim to please, sir."

"Dancing in the Moonlight?" I said. "The original by King Harvest. Not that shit cover by Toploader."

"Very good, sir. How can I help you today?"

"I would like to upgrade my operating system. I have been getting complaints."

"Very good, sir. Well, you have come to the right place. Can you tell me what you are looking for in an operating system upgrade?"

I thought about it for a while.

"Well, Keith, apparently I don't RSVP. I get invited to parties and events and just throw the invitation in the garbage."

"Ah, yes," said Keith.

"And the word is I have a tendency to talk about myself and not ask other people about their lives."

"Ah, yes," said Keith.

"And I think I heard something about thank you notes. I'm not even sure what that means."

"Ah, yes," said Keith.

"And of course the insults. It would be nice to maybe cut down a little on the insults."

"If I may," said Keith, "might I recommend a jump to Ronnie 2.0? I believe it has all the features you need. It is a very robust operating system. And, for a limited time, it comes with our new state-of-the-art filtering system at no additional charge."

"Filtering system?"

"Yes. Perfect for your, ahem, insulting situation. It filters your thoughts before they get to your mouth. Very effective."

It sounded perfect. Ronnie 2.0.

"Do you take Visa?" I asked.

"Of course, sir."

"Well, Keith. Wrap her up."

On Wednesday the Pratzers invited me for Saturday lunch. I told them thank you, I would be delighted to come.

Elan said I could confirm on Friday afternoon. Just to let him know. Malka was making her Alleppo chicken.

I said I was confirming now. I would be there with bells on.

Elan said, "Okay. But please don't cancel."

I said I would not dream of it.

On Friday, I arranged for a bouquet of flowers to be delivered to the Pratzer house. Then I went to the liquor store and bought a bottle of Elan's favorite scotch.

On Saturday, I arrived right on time. I was wearing a collared shirt and khakis. I was wearing shoes. I had brought my own head covering.

Malka thanked me for the flowers.

I shouldn't have.

I smiled. It was my pleasure.

Ronnie 2.0.

The Pratzers had invited another couple—Rose and Simon Rosenthal. They arrived a little late for my liking, but Malka had some very good snacks and Elan and I had a glass of scotch while we waited. The Rosenthals had just come back from a cruise in Croatia, and Simon was telling an excruciatingly long and boring story which I think had something to do with the buffet table.

"Tell me more about Dubrovnik," I said.

One of their kids was getting married. There was much talk about the arrangements. The hall, the food, the band.

Much much talk.

"What did you decide for centerpieces?" I asked.

After dinner, I helped clear the plates. I had never seen the Pratzers' kitchen before.

"Let me help you with that," I told Malka.

She asked if I were drunk.

I did not mention Ronnie 2.0.

Malka made her world-famous brownies. They were delish.

Malka told Rose she looked great. Was she still doing Pilates?

"Yes," said Rose. "But I really need to lose 10 pounds before the wedding."

I said, "Then maybe you should limit yourself to only one helping of brownies."

I called the 1-800 number from the car. Sly and the Family Stone. Their wait music was phenomenal. It could be a Spotify playlist.

Georgia answered after eight minutes.

"Georgia here, how can I help you?"

"Georgia," I said, "any chance I can speak to Keith?"

"I'm afraid not, sir. But I'm sure I can help you. What's your account number?"

I gave Georgia my account number.

"Is it okay if I put you on hold?"

I said it would be my pleasure.

A live version of Springsteen's Lost in the Flood. Was heartbroken when Georgia returned.

"I have it right here, sir. I see you recently upgraded your operating system to Ronnie 2.0. Are you happy with the upgrade?"

"Georgia, I am very happy with the upgrade. I am having a little more coffee with people who I genuinely despise, but all in all it has been very satisfactory."

"Well I am very happy to hear that, sir. What then seems to be the problem?"

"I just told a woman that if she wanted to lose weight, maybe she should eat a little less cake."

"Oh, dear."

"Yes."

"Well, you should maybe consider adding—oh, oh, I see here you did get our filter upgrade for free."

"I did, Georgia. It appears to be defective."

"Oh dear, yes. I am going to speak to my manager. Is it okay if I put you on hold for a second?"

"Indeed," I said.

BB King. The Thrill is Gone. Live from the Cook County Jail. God bless Georgia. I got to listen to the entire song.

"Sir?"

"Yes, Georgia."

"Well, I had a chat with my manager, and we think you may have received a refurbished filter upgrade. I'll be honest with you. They have a tendency to be a little buggy."

"Tendency to be a little buggy?"

"Yes. You aren't the first to complain. It goes along perfectly fine for a while and then the filter gets disabled. Which then disables the default filter too, so you are left with no filter at all. It's the damnest thing. But I am going to send you a brand new version. No charge."

I said fine.

Georgia said the only thing is I would have to reinstall the entire operating system again. I said no problem.

I called Malka and asked her for the Rosenthals' address. She said I should leave the Rosenthals alone. Rose was very upset. I said I was determined to make it right. She said no. I said please.

Turns out the Rosenthals lived around the corner from me.

I went to Bed Bath & Beyond and bought Rose a $300 mega-basket of soaps and oils. Then I went to the liquor store and bought Simon four bottles of Barolo, which were so expensive I had never bought them for myself. Then I went to the Judaica store and bought the newlyweds-to-be a sterling silver menorah as an engagement present.

Arms ladened with gifts, I rang the Rosenthal doorbell with my forehead. Rose was not happy to see me.

"Rose," I said, "I just wanted to tell you how sorry I am. My words were inexcusable, but I hope you can find it in your heart to forgive me. I made a completely inappropriate insensitive joke and I am so, so sorry."

I did not mention the refurbished filter software.

"An engagement present for the kids," I said, as I thrusted the sterling silver menorah into her arms.

"Well, that is really considerate of you," she said. "Shira adores sterling silver." Shira was her daughter.

"And this basket is for you."

Then Simon showed up in the doorway and relieved me of my king's ransom of Barolo. He invited me in for a scotch.

"I was just putting together this IKEA bookshelf," he said.

So I spent the next two hours with Simon Rosenthal building an IKEA bookshelf and listening to him talk about his birdwatching escapades.

"Which is your favorite owl?" I asked.

Rose and Shira Rosenthal spent the entire two hours fighting about the menu. Apparently, Shira Rosenthal would rather die than serve fish at her wedding. She repeated the line, "Fuck them if they don't eat steak," about six times.

"She's quite the firecracker," said Simon Rosenthal about his daughter.

"I love her passion for meat," I said.

Then I spent an hour looking at bridesmaid dress pictures.

"You can never go wrong with periwinkle blue," I said.

When Shira's fiancé, Benjamin, arrived, she complained that he was late and clearly had no interest in any of the wedding preparations. She pointed at me and said, "He has done more than you and he isn't even invited!" Then she browbeat him to thank me for the sterling silver menorah I had brought them as an engagement present.

Ben shook my hand, and said thank you.

I said it was my pleasure.

Then I said, "Why would you want to spend the rest of your life with that bitch?"

I didn't waste my time with a customer service person this time. I asked to speak to the manager.

Her name was Marjorie.

"Here's what I think happened," said Marjorie after I gave her my account number. "I have seen this happen before."

"Marjorie," I said gently, "your filter is a piece of shit. Excuse my French."

"I understand your frustration," said Marjorie. "But I'm pretty sure we'll have a good laugh about it after."

I didn't think we would.

Neither the Rosenthals nor Pratzers were now talking to me.

"You see, what I think happened is that when you downloaded the new operating system, the one with the brand new filter, you actually first forgot to delete the old version. The one with the refurbished filter. So the old operating system remained as the default system. Did you forget to delete the old operating system?"

"Marjorie," I said. "Nobody told me to first delete the old operating system."

"It is a common mistake. Happens all the time. Here's what I'm going to do for you. I think you will really be happy."

I didn't think I would, but there was not much I could do. I told Marjorie that I was listening.

"I am going to have to get the okay from the general manager for this, but I am going to tell him it is a special circumstance, and I am going to, honestly this never happens, I am going to upgrade you to Ronnie 3.0. With, of course, a brand new top-of-the-line filter. What do you think of that?"

I told Marjorie I thought that sounded fine.

Marjorie asked if it was okay if she put me on hold while she asked her general manager.

I said no problem.

Marjorie must have had a lengthy discussion with her general manager, because I listened to Dylan's Blood on the Tracks in its entirety while I waited.

Great album.

The general manager approved of Ronnie 3.0. Marjorie said, "Don't forget to delete the old version."

Ronnie 3.0 was a gamechanger.

The Rosenthals issued a restraining order. Five hundred feet. But that did not stop me from buying Ben and Shira a 2020 Audi SQ5 as a wedding present. And I bought Rose and Simon and Elan and Malka a two-week Caribbean cruise.

My niece Rachie called and she wanted her old Uncle Ronnie back. She begged me to return to Ronnie 1.0.

I said that Ronnie 1.0 was an insensitive, rude curmudgeon.

She said she missed him. She wanted him back.

I said, "Ronnie 1.0 had the original filter. One never knew what I might say."

She said she missed him. She wanted him back.

I said, "Ronnie 1.0 never committed to anything. Always waited to see if something better came along."

She said she missed him. She wanted him back.

I said, "Okay. Love you." I would call the 1-800 number.

She said, "Love you."

I called the 1-800 number.

They put me on hold.

Funeral for a Friend by Elton John.

Love that song.

My call waiting went off about halfway through the song.

It was Rachie.

"Hey, Uncle Ronnie," said Rachie.

I said, "Hey, Rachie."

And she said, "Maybe see if they have Ronnie 1.5."

I said, "Okay."

LABRADOODLE

Photograph © Susanne906 / pixabay.com

I wouldn't be picking up dog shit with a small plastic bag if I could have remembered if it was garbage day or recycling day.

Check that.

I wouldn't be picking up dog shit with a small plastic bag if I could have just remembered to keep my mouth shut.

The street I live on in Toronto alternates between recycling and garbage each week. I guess every street in Toronto is like that.

On our street, the pickup is on Thursdays.

I am pretty good at remembering on Wednesday night that there is a pickup the next morning. What I am not so good at remembering is whether it is garbage or recycling. I don't know why. I just can't do it.

I can recite all 50 states.

I can, if you give me a minute, even remember all 50 state capitals.

But damn if I can remember if it is garbage or recycling.

So what I usually do is walk over to the neighbours and check which bin they have put out. The recycling bin is blue and the garbage bin is gray but from a distance they kind of look the same, so I have to actually walk over and check for myself. The problem is my neighbour on my left doesn't put out the bin until early morning—which doesn't work for me. And the neighbour on my right—a lovely old Scottish man—has been wrong twice. Which meant four weeks until my overflowing garbage bin gets picked up.

Not a pretty scene.

So I usually end up crossing the street. The family who lives there puts out the bins early and never gets it wrong. They too are a lovely family with two small kids who have been my cross-the-street neighbours for nearly five years.

And I can't remember their names.

Am sure I knew their names at one point and may have even been reminded. But I now had no clue.

Which would be okay if not for the fact that every time I saw the husband, he greeted me with an enthusiastic, "Hey, Ron." Like he was trying to stick it to me.

On that particular Wednesday night, the coast looked clear, so I quickly crossed the street to take a peek—recycling—I fucking knew that and was making a hasty retreat when I heard the screen door open and heard his cheerful, "Hey, Ron."

I had recently defaulted to, "Hey, neighbour," but I knew he knew that I did not know his name and every conversation was just a tiny bit uncomfortable. This one was not any different but it was short and would have been totally innocuous had it not led to me picking up dog shit with a small plastic bag.

He asked me how things were and did not wait for my reply when he announced that they were going to get a dog.

I said, "Oh, yeah."

And he said yeah. The wife wasn't totally on board, but the kids had been really on their case and what with all that was going on and the distance learning and everything, he thought they deserved it even though the wife wasn't totally on board.

And I said, "Oh, yeah."

Then he said they were thinking of a labradoodle.

Did I know what that was?

I did, but he proceeded to tell me anyway.

He finished explaining the hybrid process and the breeder in Milton they were getting it from and then waited for me to say something.

So I said that I was thinking of getting a dog.

Although I wasn't.

"That's great," he said. "Have you decided what kind? Have you lined up a breeder?"

And I said, "I'm not really a breeder type of guy."

Although I was.

"I think I will probably get a rescue. You know what they say—'adopt, don't shop.'"

I didn't know who said that. I had no idea where I had even heard it.

But, for some reason, it shut him up, and I managed to cross the street back to my house and drag my recycling bin to the curb.

And that should have ended things and kept me far away from dog shit and small inverted plastic bags, and it would have if Mrs. Katsakis had not died.

Mrs. Katsakis was a Greek lady who lived three doors down. She tended her garden most days. In 10 years, I had never spoken to her. I may have waved at her thrice. She lived three doors down. In my world, it was as if she lived in Myanmar.

I did not know her name.

She was the Greek lady who lived three doors down.

I would not have known her name if my neighbour from across the street had not knocked on my door and said, "Hey, Ron, Mrs. Katsakis has died."

I did not know who Mrs. Katsakis was, but I didn't really know any other Greek ladies, and there was no other Greek lady that the neighbour across the street and I had in common, so I was able to piece it together.

I mean, I wasn't a complete idiot.

I'm not sure why my neighbour from across the street thought I needed to know about Mrs. Katsakis. I mean, it was sad and all, but I wasn't sure what it had to do with me. I figured maybe he was collecting some money because I never saw anyone visiting her and she lived in this small bungalow, and even though I didn't know her from Adam, I was happy to do my part, especially if it helped get rid of my neighbour from across the street.

So I said, "Hold on, let me go get my checkbook," even though he hadn't said anything about money and had really only told me that Mrs. Katsakis had died.

I retreated into my house when he said:

"She had a dog."

And I said, "Oh, yeah."

And he said, "Yeah. And I remember you saying you were thinking of getting a dog."

And I said, "Oh, yeah."

And he said, "Yeah. You said you wanted to adopt. Her children live in Vancouver. There is no one to take the dog. So I thought of you. I mean, it feels like serendipity."

Serendipity.

It felt like he was trying to stick it to me.

I asked him what kind of dog.

"A Scottish Terrier. Her name is Olympus."

Olympus. Jesus, Mary and Joseph.

So now I am walking my new dog down the street. Olympus. Stopping from time to time to pick up the shit with a small plastic bag.

I am scooping up the shit when I suddenly remember my neighbour's name:

Ethan.

Fuck.

I should have remembered that.

It is Wednesday night and Ethan has his garbage bins out. I drop the bag of shit into his bin.

Then I cross the street and go home with my dog.

DROPPING A SKI

There's not much to like about getting old, but one of the perks is I no longer do things in order to impress women. It is a pleasure. I say this to Caroline, my sister-in-law. She says I should still consider trimming my nose hair.

Anyway, this story is about a time back in the day when I cared about impressing women. It is about a woman named Connie Hillerman. It is a little bit about my friend Mike. And it is a little bit about friendship.

I haven't thought about this story for a long time, and I only mention it because today my niece Rena asked me why I have never waterskied. I told her I used to waterski. She said, "I am 17 and have never seen you waterski." Am sure she is right. At some point in my life, waterskiing fell into the 'nothing good can come of this' category. It has been safely and securely stowed in that category for many years. I would like to say I figured that out on my own.

But then there wouldn't be a story to tell.

This picture is from when I was 16 or 17. I think it was taken either in Singapore or Malaysia. I love this picture because I am on one ski. It gives me a lot of flexibility in my storytelling.

I learned to waterski on the Changi River in Singapore on Saturday mornings with my friends Phil, Mike, and Paul. Phil was an expert waterskier. I think he could barefoot. Mike 'borrowed' his mom's car. Paul 'borrowed' his mom's credit card. Am quite sure none of us had a driver's license. Then we rented a ski boat for a few hours. Phil taught us how to get up and then eventually how to drop a ski. I could do a shallow water beach start on one ski, but the deepwater single ski takeoff was always a challenge. I could do it one time in five and eventually gave up trying entirely. Especially since we were renting by the hour and wasting time trying to get up was not a good idea. I stuck to the drop—which I got pretty good at.

There was, to be honest, something a little magical about dropping a ski. You would put on the drop ski and leave it tight enough so it wouldn't fly off when you got up on two but loose enough so you could easily slip out of it. You would ask the driver to make a short loop, get back on the straightaway in front of the dock or beach where you would drop the ski so it could be easily retrieved—put all your weight on the other ski. Then deftly slip out and shake off the drop ski, hover over the water for a few seconds, then carefully find the strap on the back of the remaining ski with your toes. Find your balance. And ta-da! You were now on one ski. I always found everything after that a bit anti-climactic. I could slalom, albeit with not much of a shoulder dip, through the wake well enough, but I was always pretty quick to touch my head, signalling I wanted to go back home. Unlike my nieces, I was never one to complain that my turn was too short.

There was always something exciting and even a little bit dangerous about those Saturday morning ski trips. I remember we got up early, met in a designated spot, drove for 45 minutes, skied for two hours, then breakfasted on roadside chilli crab eating quickly so we could get the car back before Mike's mom woke up from her late night slumber. Am sure she knew but, if she did, she never let on. Still, there was just something about a trip with a stolen car which added to the salt of the water, the speed of the boat, and spiciness of the chilli crab.

I don't really remember waterskiing after Singapore. If I did, it might have been a couple of times at the most. Then we began renting cottages in the summer. Up on Healey Lake in Muskoka. The cottage came with access to a 65 hp ski boat. We waterskied and took the kids on tube rides all summer. My brother and I became pretty good ski boat drivers. We also skied, but we turned into those waterski assholes who only ski when the lake was pristine. When it was glass. Other times, well, other times were for the other people. Those who didn't know any better. The irony is neither of us were really any good. I know I never really got better. And to develop into a good skier you really had to have no fear.

I had a lot of fear.

Falling was not so fun.

Faceplants.

Skis hitting you in the head.

To get better, you had to take chances. And if you took chances, you would fall.

And falling was not so much fun.

So, we skied.

But we didn't really have our hearts in it.

We both kinda remember the day when we decided that maybe waterskiing wasn't for us. We had gotten up early on a morning which maybe was a tiny bit too chilly to ski. We both had very short perfunctory runs. At one point, he turned to me and said, "Do you like this?" I said, "Not so much." "Yeah," he said. "Me neither."

So we didn't stop cold turkey. But it was no longer all that interesting. We still talked the talk but didn't walk the walk.

Which is a perfectly good explanation and what I could have told my niece Rena but she is a smart cookie and would have figured there was more to the story. She would have wanted to hear about Connie Hillerman.

Connie Hillerman is a woman I used to have a thing for. If you have read any of my stories, you have already guessed she did not have a thing for me. That is fine. Connie Hillerman, truth be told, was not that great. She wore a lot of white t-shirts. I think it might have been the only thing she ever wore. Back in the day, a white t-shirt was generally good enough for me.

Connie Hillerman had a best friend with an unfortunate old-fashioned alliteration name—Mildred MacIntire. Mildred, 'don't call me Millie,' was a real sweetheart, salt-of-the-earth, shirt-off-your-back kind of gal. I don't know what she was like when she was young, but the burden of that name eventually wore her down and she became, in fact, she embodied, the name.

I'm not saying that was a bad thing.

I'm just saying.

Mildred MacIntire had a thing for my friend Mike.

I think you can see where this is going.

So when I suggested a Labor Day weekend getaway up at the Aston Resort on Lake Muskoka for the four of us, Connie Hillerman was looking out for her friend Mildred MacIntire and Mike, well, Mike was looking out for me.

Now the thing I like best about Mike, apart from being a true and loyal friend, is that he is the epitome of a glass-half-full kind of guy. I too am a glass-half-full kind of guy, but my glass just happens to be half-full of arsenic. Mike has the uncanny ability to make the best of any situation. It is true it often involved a libation of sorts, but that did not take away from his very good disposition.

So you can imagine how desperate the scene was on late Sunday afternoon as we sunned ourselves on the dock, Connie Hillerman having exchanged her white t-shirt for a white bikini, when Mike turned to me and said, "It isn't going very well."

It was a bit of an understatement.

Connie Hillerman had adopted an attitude that could best be described as bored disdain.

She did not find me funny.

She did not find me charming.

She did not find, nor did she even try to look for, any redeeming qualities whatsoever.

Bored disdain.

Which is why Mike and I, and also Mildred MacIntire, were taken aback when Connie Hillerman popped up from her deck chair and exclaimed, "Wow, that is so fucking cool!"

We looked up to see what she was talking about. Her enthusiasm, which up to this point had been less than non-existent, made me think that maybe a whale had surfaced on the lake. But all I could see was a ski boat and water skiers.

I turned to cautiously ask her what she was talking about, but she was still looking out, enthralled, at the lake. I tried to formulate a question but Mildred MacIntire beat me to the punch.

"What," she asked, "is so fucking cool?"

"Did you see how he dropped a ski?" said Connie Hillerman in a voice I would give up a month of Sundays to hear just once. "He was skiing on two skis and then he dropped one and continued on one. That is so fucking cool!"

I don't really know all that much about Connie Hillerman outside of her penchant for white t-shirts. I can't really say why she thought it was cool. Maybe she had never seen people waterskiing before. Maybe she had grown up in the desert and had not experienced boating and waterskiing. It's not for me to say.

Now I have a lot of friends. They are, for the most part, good, kind-hearted people. But I think the vast majority would have turned to Connie Hillerman and told her, each in their own way, that dropping a ski was really considered almost the lowest echelon of water skiing skills. Most would have declared they had learned to drop a ski at the age of eight. That dropping a ski was no big whup.

My friend Mike, however, is not most people.

He turned to Connie Hillerman and said:

"My boy Ronnie can drop a ski."

Now I don't know if Connie Hillerman believed Mike. She knew he was my proverbial wingman. That he would probably do and say anything to get me a foot closer to her white t-shirts. So am not sure what was going through her head. All I know is she turned to me, looking at me for the first time that weekend and said, "Show me."

Look, I'm not an idiot. I knew that dropping a ski was not going to suddenly transform me from a poor shmuck to a knight in dull armor. But I badly needed a win. Any win.

I couldn't remember the last time I had skied, but I could drop a ski in my sleep. It was, despite what Connie Hillerman thought, really no big whup.

So I tightened my bathing suit and walked with what I hoped was my own version of bored disdain to the end of the pier where I gave my room number so they could charge me for the ski.

I took my place in line but it turned out I didn't have to wait long. I was up next.

The kid driving the boat had zinc on his nose and a bronzed face. He looked like he was 12.

"Quick loop," I said. "Am going to drop right in front." I pointed to where Mike, Mildred MacIntire and Connie Hillerman were now standing, closer to the water's edge.

The kid said, "White bikini?" Maybe he wasn't 12 after all. I said, "Yup." He said, "Okay."

I bobbed in the water, the ill-fitting life jacket raising up to my neck. I realized I needed to pee but this probably wasn't the time or place. For a split second, I worried about getting up on two skis, but that worry quickly evaporated. Next thing I was up, adjusting my bathing suit and preparing for the sharp turn.

The plan was to drop, make a few cuts, and call it a day. Piece of cake.

I stayed behind the wake as the boat made the turn and then began testing shifting my weight as we neared the dock.

I was not the least bit nervous.

The ski slipped off easily. I had set the tension up perfectly.

I heard a cheer from the bank.

I then brought my toe back in order to wedge it into the back strap.

This is where things got a little interesting.

You see, if you are skiing on two skis, you usually get a matched pair. But if your plan is to drop a ski, one of the skis is the slalom ski, which has a back strap for your second foot. The other ski, the drop ski, doesn't have that strap.

But that isn't the ski I had just dropped in front of Connie Hillerman and her white bikini. I had just dropped the slalom ski.

So when I reached back to place my free foot in the back strap, I could not find the back strap.

Because there was no back strap.

When I started this story, I said it was about Connie Hillerman, about my friend Mike, and a little bit about friendship. I should have added it was also about hubris.

Because when I couldn't find the back strap, what I should have done is let go of the rope. It was the smart thing to do. It was the only thing to do. But although I couldn't find the back strap, I did manage to place my foot rather comfortably and surprisingly easily on the back of the ski.

I was skiing on one ski.

I could do this.

Until the boat turned.

When the boat turned, my entire body turned with the boat. Well, my entire body except for the leg attached to the foot which wasn't attached to the back strap. That went a different way.

Mike, who is a glass-half-full kind of guy, likes to remind me that when I made the splits in the water, resulting in a class-three groin pull, at least I did it out of sight of Connie Hillerman. At least that was some consolation.

You gotta love Mike.

So I tell Rena why I don't waterski anymore. She laughs at all the right parts but mostly wants to know what happened to Connie Hillerman. I say, "I don't know. We all lost touch." She says, "That's what Facebook is for." It takes Rena two minutes to find her. She is still friends with Mildred MacIntire.

"She's cute," says Rena. "She's really cute. Do you want to see?"

I say no. I don't want to see.

"She's divorced," says Rena. "Three kids."

She looks up at me and we have a staring contest. She knows she is going to win. She always wins.

"Okay. Hand me the phone," I say.

Connie Hillerman still looks good. I scroll down. A lot of pictures of her in white t-shirts.

I get up and go to the bathroom in my brother's bedroom. I open the medicine cabinet. It takes me a while but I finally find what I am looking for.

Nose hair trimmers.

THE GONG

Photograph © Todd Rosenberg / Todd Rosenberg Photography

Of all of the stories I have ever written, the only one which has ever give me pause is the Heather Lewis Movie Theatre story. Since the only people who ever read these pieces are friends and family, you might already be familiar with it. If not, I will give you a brief refresher: it is about the time I went to a movie with Heather Lewis, left ten minutes into the movie in order to go to the bathroom, then poked my head into another theatre where I ended up standing in the back for the entire movie. It is a funny story and I'm not sure the description does it justice but it does do a pretty good job of conveying the fact that it makes me look like a little bit of an asshole.

The story works on its own but in the collection it was preceded by a handful of other stories in which my friend Allie implored me not to tell the Heather Lewis Movie Theatre story in a social setting because it makes me look like a little bit of an asshole. I thought, and so did others, that it was a pretty good payoff after a well crafted set up and it became a fan favorite. Also, although there were plenty of other stories which made me look like a little bit of an asshole there were some which cast me in a favorable light so I figured it would all balance out.

So it should have been fine but although I had disguised her name and changed details, I still had a feeling in the back of my mind that Heather Lewis would somehow get pissed off. There was absolutely no reason why she should get pissed off because she comes off looking good and I come off looking like a dick but I had a bad feeling about it and so, operating under the an abundance of caution credo, I decided to remove it, and the stories which referenced it, out of the collection.

I self publish my books using Amazon's Print-On-Demand program so changing the book file, which I ended up doing quite often, was a very easy exercise.

I'm not sure what the opposite of best seller is but that is the category I fit in so there could not have been more than two dozen people with a copy of the book which included the Heather Lewis Movie Theatre story.

That is only to say that when I ran into Heather Lewis outside of the Baskin Robbins on Avenue, my heart did not go to my throat because I did not for a second think she would have read any of my stories and least of all the Heather Lewis Movie Theatre story. We greeted each other enthusiastically, although we neither hugged or kissed, and she asked me what was going on and I said 'same old, same old' which seem to satisfy her even though I had no idea what she thought my 'same old, same old' was and it certainly wasn't writing about the time I left her alone in the movie theatre. She was very excited to tell me about the fundraiser for the Toronto Symphony she was co-chairing. There was, she said excitedly, going to be an amazing silent auction.

Heather Lewis had always been a big fan of classical music and we had gone to quite a few concerts on our dates. People are surprised to learn that I too am a classical music enthusiast- the first record albums our family ever owned was the ten set Herbert von Karajan with the Berlin Philharmonic. I had been weaned on classical music. Also, I think myself a bit of a renaissance man and knowledge and appreciation of the classics was an important building block.

And that was that. We said our goodbyes and all would have been well and good and I would not have ended with a Heather Lewis story which made the Heather Lewis Movie Theatre story look like a walk in the park if she hadn't, as she turned to leave, a dripping mint chocolate chip cone in hand, said "I thought the movie theatre story was cute."

"Tell me again exactly what she said," said Allie. We were sitting on my back deck eating party sandwiches from St. Urbain. I had already told the story three times.

"She said 'I thought the movie theatre story was cute.'"

Back in the day Allie and a team of forensic scientists would have come over to my apartment in order to analyze and parse a message a woman might have left on my answering machine. But I had no message. I could only relay what I heard.

"Was she smiling?"

"No."

"Was she smirking?"

"No. She said it straight up. No intonation."

"Let me ask you this," she said "if 100 people had heard her how many of them would have thought she was saying anything other than she thought it was cute?"

"Am I one of the 100?" I asked.

"No," she replied.

"Then I don't think anyone would read anything in it."

"But you do?"

"It is Heather Lewis. I dunno. Doesn't feel right."

"Did it ever occur to you that nobody gives a shit about your stories?"

"That is just crazy talk."

"So what are you going to do?"

"I'm going to the Symphony Fundraiser. To the silent auction. I'm going to bid on something expensive."

"That might be the dumbest thing you have ever done."

But she was wrong.

I was about to get a lot dumber.

Here's what you should do in order to test the strength of your friendships. Buy a table of ten seats to a symphony fundraiser and see how many people are willing to get dressed in a tuxedo or evening gown for an evening of free food and selected pieces from Chopin.

I was now up to two.

Lewberg, after I checked to see if the bar would stock Ketel One and Goldfarb, after I reassured him that I would pay for his rented tuxedo, that the food was indeed free and, this was the clincher, he could wear earplugs throughout.

Everyone else said no.

Most laughed in my face.

In the end, I donated the extra 7 seats back to the foundation and Lewberg, Goldfarb and I found ourselves sitting with a busload of elderly residents from a local retirement home.

"Heather Lewis looks good," said Lewberg.

Goldfarb took his earplugs out and said "what?"

"Heather Lewis look good," Lewberg said again.

It was true. Heather Lewis did look good. We had waved from across the room but had not spoken.

Lewberg refused to analyze the wave with me.

"Heather Lewis is not pissed off at you," he said. "She doesn't know you are alive. Seriously. Nobody cares about your stories."

"Yeah, I'm sure you are right," I said.

"How much was the table?" Asked Goldfarb.

"Two grand," I replied.

"How many books have you sold?" He asked.

"Last count 84." I said.

"Your business skills are inspirational," said Goldfarb.

"I'm going to go bid on something," I said.

"Yeah. Go spend some money," said Goldfarb. "That wave looked angry." He then put his ear plugs back on.

Goldfarb, Lewberg and Allie were right. Heather Lewis was not pissed off at all. It was all in my mind. But, there was an item in the silent auction I was actually interested in. It was a guest appearance with the Toronto Symphony during a performance of Rossini's Barber of Seville.

Playing the gong.

Two strikes.

Da dum.

The Barber of Seville was my late father's favorite piece. When the gong played, he would punch the air.

Da dum.

It became a thing in our family.

Da dum.

It was as close as my Egyptian Jewish family came to a Bruce Springsteen concert during Born to Run. The gong da dum in the middle of Rossini's Barber of Seville.

Da dum.

So, I had kinda forgotten about Heather Lewis. But now, I wanted to play the gong.

I won't tell you how much I bid.

Let's just say I will have to sell more than 84 books.

Gustave Klimsh made it clear he was not happy to have me playing the gong in his symphony.

He was the conductor of the Toronto Symphony. He said his orchestra was made up of the most talented and dedicated musicians in the world. He did not need it sullied by a former powder paint salesman.

He didn't actually say that

But it was what I felt.

"Look." I am happy to bow out. I love this piece. I wouldn't want to do anything to ruin it."

"No. No. You will play. It is a gong. You cant fuck it up."

He didn't actually say that.

But it is what I felt.

I knew the piece backwards and forwards.

On the day of the first rehearsal, I paid close attention and hit the gong right after the third arpeggio.

Da dum.

I nailed it.

Then Gustave said "No."

And then I said "No?"

"It is one gong," he said.

And I said "I think it is two." Then I said "da dum."

And he said, a little more sternly this time "it is one gong."

I said "I have been listening to Herbert van Karajan and the Berlin Philharmonic all week I am pretty sure it is two."

"Van Karajan does not understand Rossini," he spat out "it is one. You will do one."

Then the second cellist turned to me and said "Just do what he says."

So I did one. It sounded wrong. But I did one. We rehearsed all week. Truth be told, it became incredibly boring. If I could do it again, I would have bid on the spa weekend.

But on the day of the concert, Heather Lewis announced me as the guest percussionist. Gustave gave me a wave and the musicians tapped their bows as they do on these occasions. I have to admit, it felt pretty good.

So, when I did what I did, I did it out of reflex and not spite or bitterness.

It was my father punching the air.

Da dum.

Now a lot of people who aren't familiar with classical music think that conducting is a ceremonial position. That the conductor is just waving his baton around in order to look dramatic. But when a conductor stops conducting, it is a little like taking your foot off the pedal.

And when I did da dum, Gustave stopped conducting. Just for a split second.

And so the musicians stopped playing.

Just for a split second.

I'm sure most of the people didn't even notice.

Although Heather Lewis did.

Sitting in the front row.

So if you are reading this story can you please do me a favor and don't show it to Heather Lewis.

I have a feeling she won't think it is cute.

THE THINGS I KNOW

Photograph © John Weinhardt / Unsplash

I have a text from Mike. 'Hey Ron, call me. I have a good story. Better than Dubrovnik.'

I understand what he is referring to.

For many years, I used to make restaurant reservations under the name Dubrovnik. This was long before the breakup of the former Yugoslavia and certainly long before the Croatian seaside resort became a *de riguer* destination for tourists.

I don't know why I picked the name. My family name is neither difficult to remember nor to pronounce. I liked the sound of it. And I liked I knew of its existence. And who could not take pleasure in hearing the hostess call out: "Dubrovnik, party of six. Your table is ready."

Dubrovnik.

It's just something I know.

Another thing I know is the capital of Burkina Faso. It is Ouagadougou. One of the great all-time names. It is also just fun to say. Go ahead and say it.

I also know Burkina Faso used to be called Upper Volta.

I know Timbuktu is a real place.

I know where it is. It is in Mali. I know it is not the capital, which by the way, is Bamako.

Another great name.

Timbuktu has a special place in my heart because it is featured in one of my father's favourite poems.

Tim and I a hunting went,
When we came across three women in a tent.
As they were three and we were two,
I bucked one and Timbuktu.

Am not sure how my father, a scientist and intellectual who spoke seven languages, ever came to this poem, but he loved it and would start laughing, displaying his crooked teeth, well before the final line.

I know the longest word in the world.

pneumonoultramicroscopicsilicovolcanoconiosis.

And I still know how to spell it.

Cross my heart.

I know the name and height of the tallest mountain in North America. Denali in Alaska. 20,320 feet. I know it used to be called Mount McKinley.

I know how to convert centigrade to Fahrenheit.

I know all the words of the Lord's Prayer.

I know who Yossarian is. I know both Franny and Zooey.

I know Elton John used to be called Reginald Dwight and Bob Dylan was originally Robert Allen Zimmerman.

As the son of a chemical engineer, I know that N is nitrogen and Na is sodium.

I know Napoleon was exiled in Elba and died in St. Helena.

I know the names of the two catchers on the 1969 Montreal Expos.

John Bateman.

John Boccabella.

Another fun word to say.

These are some of the things I still know.

But so does Siri. So does Google. In a matter of seconds, anyone and everyone in the world can know as much as me. That and so much more. Truth be told, what I know is of no use. Has no value. What has value today is knowing how to find the things you do not know.

But I can't seem to delete the things I know and put them in the trash in order to make room for other, more useful things, like, for example, where I have left my keys.

So like the expired condom in my wallet, I carry them around without any expectation I will ever need to use them.

I call Mike back. He is a dentist in Ottawa. He launches into his story without exchanging any pleasantries.

"So I have a new patient in the chair the other day. She's come in for a checkup. She has an accent, so I ask her where she's from. She says, get this, from Burkino Faso. I almost wet myself from excitement. Have been waiting nearly 30 years for this moment."

"Jesus, you lucky bastard. So, what did you do?"

"I played it cool for a second. Examined a couple of her back molars and then said, real casual-like, 'I heard Ouagadougou is beautiful in the spring.' She almost fell off the chair!"

"Oh my god. Unbelievable. I am so jealous."

"It was beautiful, Ron. Better than I had imagined. Hope it happens to you one day."

I hope so too.

Until then, I can only hope the internet crashes.

THE JACKPOT

There was a golf course out near Naples Goldfarb liked to play. It was a pretty nice public course, nothing special, but it had been the only course where Goldfarb had ever broken 80, so he liked going back in the hope he might catch lightening twice.

I didn't mind the drive, but it made Lewberg crazy to drive two hours each way when we actually lived on a golf course.

"Are we at war?" he would say.

Now I love Goldfarb, he is one of my oldest and dearest friends, but he is a bit of a mope, especially because he has never once come close to breaking 80 since, and so the prospect of spending the entire day with him without having Lewberg as a buffer was not altogether enticing.

So I nudged Lewberg a little and got him to reluctantly agree to go one more time. We had a perfectly nice round, Goldfarb shot a 98, we had cheeseburgers and fries at the club, but Lewberg couldn't stop complaining about the distance and made it abundantly clear he had no intention of coming back.

I didn't really have a dog in this fight, but I pointed out it was only 120 miles and we would be home in well under two hours. And we probably would have, if Goldfarb didn't have to go to the bathroom 45 minutes after we left the golf course.

Now the road between Boca and Naples, a highway known as Alligator Alley, does not have many rest stops, and Goldfarb's pressing need was not one which could be accommodated by pulling over to the side of the road, so we took the first exit in search of that rarest of Florida attractions—a commode in the Everglades.

Lewberg, like a hound dog on the trail, sensed it before we saw it. A small neon sign on a post.

Casino—8 miles. Poker. Cheap Drinks. Swampland Jackpot now $50,000!!!!!!!!

The parking lot was full and the casino appeared like a mirage in the middle of the Everglades. Goldfarb, moving faster than we had ever seen him, made his way to the restrooms while Lewberg and I went to the bar. Lewberg, to his credit, knew that at $4 per drink, the vodka was not going to be Ketel, so we both got $2 Budweisers

We toasted Goldfarb's bowels and surveyed the scene. The place was packed. We were literally in the middle of nowhere. Where had all of these people come from?

We were on to our second $2 Buds when Goldfarb came back and ordered a beer of his own.

We knew he was about to rate the bathroom and he made his proclamation after his first swig of beer.

"Eight," he said.

An eight was huge for Goldfarb. An eight was Nirvana.

Lewberg suggested we play a few hands of poker. I said okay and Goldfarb, still basking after his successful expedition, surprisingly agreed.

The game was $3–$6 seven-card stud with a $1 ante.

Which was pretty normal.

What was not normal was that every poker table was outfitted with a poker slot machine. Set up just to the side of the dealer's chair. After everybody anted, the dealer would push a button on the slot machine and the players would wait and hope to see if the five rotating tumblers turned up a royal flush.

It was fucked up.

But it was cool. I had never seen anything like it.

Lewberg, who loved all sorts of gambling, was ecstatic. He said, "We are only one hooker away from being in heaven."

Goldfarb, who had an advanced degree in mathematics, was bemused. He recognized it for the scam it was. Because the casino took money out from each pot, and very likely much more, to fund each jackpot. A jackpot which almost never hit.

If the royal flush hit, every player who had played the hand, there were usually seven per table, would share the jackpot.

At $50,000, that worked out to about $7000 per player.

Not too shabby.

Which explained why the poker room was full.

They were pretty strict about having to ante in order to participate in the jackpot, so when someone went to the bathroom or for a walk to stretch their legs, he or she would arrange for the dealer to ante for them while they were gone.

About an hour after we sat down, Goldfarb got up to go to the bathroom again. The look on his face made it clear that his digestive system had some unfinished business.

As he got up, the dealer, the name tag said Sonny Sarasota—Sonny was his name and Sarasota was where he was from—said, "I'll take care of your ante, sir."

And Goldfarb said, "That's okay. I'm good."

And Sonny said, "If you don't ante, you don't participate in the jackpot."

Goldfarb said, "It's all good, Sonny. Just leave my chips alone."

It's not that Goldfarb was cheap. Although he was. It was just that Goldfarb was a numbers guy. And the numbers didn't add up for him. He didn't mind paying the dollar when he was in a hand, but he was damned if he was going to pay while he sat on the toilet excavating his bowels. Lewberg and I knew that. It was why we kept our mouths shut.

He glared at Lewberg and I and pointed menacingly at his chips and said, "I know how much I have."

Goldfarb left and Sonny announced, "Okay, everyone. Antes up." And we all tossed in a $1 chip. Except for a slightly heavy middle-aged Chinese woman in an elaborate floral-pattern dress, who cursed the slot machine in Chinese every time its tumblers betrayed her. She was here for the jackpot. I'm not sure she even knew how to play seven-card stud. She threw in two chips and pointed at Goldfarb's empty seat.

Sonny said, "Got it."

The slot machine brought no glory, and we all quietly played out the hand. Goldfarb was still not back. I was feeling bad for him, but at least he had rated the bathroom an eight.

Sonny announced, "Antes up."

Once again, the Chinese lady threw in two chips and again pointed to Goldfarb's empty seat. And then unleashed in Mandarin or Cantonese what I can only imagine was the most filthy and vile tirade at the slot machine.

I don't know what she said, but the tumblers revealed themselves magically and methodically.

10 of diamonds.

J of diamonds.

Q of diamonds.

K of diamonds.

Ace of diamonds.

A royal flush.

The table erupted.

The Chinese lady, Gloria, kissed Sonny. Then she kissed the slot machine.

Just then, Goldfarb came back. He looked at the flashing royal flush, then at his undisturbed stack of chips. Then back at the royal flush.

I didn't have Goldfarb's mind for numbers, but I could do the math in my head.

$7142.85 per person.

Without Goldfarb, it would have been $8333.33 per person. But not a single person begrudged the extra share. To a player, including me, and certainly Lewberg, who was now slow-dancing with the Chinese lady, we all believed the extra chip brought the luck we needed to hit the jackpot.

I believed it then.

I still believe it now

Lewberg and I would have been happy to let Goldfarb suffer for a few hours, but Sonny let him off the hook. He told him that Gloria, I guess she was a regular, had paid the ante and he would participate in the jackpot

Goldfarb, who really wasn't used to things working out for him, turned to Gloria and stood up very straight. He addressed her in a very formal manner.

"Madam," he said, "your act was one of the kindest and most generous I have ever encountered in my entire life."

The Chinese lady detangled herself from Lewberg, stood up very straight herself, and then spoke the first words of English we had heard her speak all night:

"You owe me $2, asshole."

A GOOD OPENING SENTENCE

Vintage photograph, Germany

The first time Amanda caught fire was the summer she was living on the top floor of a big house on Clinton Street with the drummer of a Leonard Cohen cover band called Eating on Yom Kippur, which was made up almost exclusively of ex-rabbinical students who had been expelled from a local Yeshiva for selling amphetamines to their fellow classmates.

That's all I have. I found one page in my blue folder. With one lonely opening sentence. I have no idea what the story was going to be about. I like the opening line though. I thought it deserved to see the light of day.

For my money, the best opening line is Mark Helprin's from his short story *The Schreuderspitze:*

In Munich are many men who look like weasels.

I just love that.

The second line from that story is no slouch either.

Whether by genetic accident, meticulous cross breeding, an early and puzzling migration, coincidence, or a reason we do not know, they exist in great numbers.

To hell with it. I have to give you the entire paragraph because it is so fucking good.

Remarkably, they accentuate this unfortunate tendency by wearing mustaches, Alpine hats, and tweed. A man who resembles a rodent should never wear tweed.

I just love that!

I like a good opening line. It sets the tone. Makes you sit up and take notice.

On the other hand, a good opening line can be a burden. It sets the bar too high. I don't really remember the rest of Helprin's story. But I don't think it is as good as the opening. How could it?

I often quit after writing what I think is a good opening. I admire it for a while. Reread it a few times. Send it to friends for their approval. 'Damn, that's good,' I might say to myself. And then I quit and go about my day. Because, you know, writing is hard.

My friend Tuddy remembers most of what I have written. His favorite is *I go to the library and take out books I know I will not read. Classics mostly.*

I like that. I mean, it's not Helprin. But I like it. I don't think there was any actual story. If there was, it was forgettable.

A good opening line is a bit like a party trick. It is all smoke and mirrors. I do a lot of that in my life. I can play the opening bars of

Bill Withers' Lean on Me on the piano. Sounds pretty good. It is the only thing I know how to play on the piano.

A good opening line is a bit like flexing your muscles. You aren't actually doing any heavy lifting. You are just giving the impression that you can.

My pride and joy was my Hemingway-esque opening for yet another unwritten story. It was a thing of beauty.

Get this:

It was a hot muggy night in Barcelona and all the good whores had the flu.

Jesus that is good.

How do I come up with that. It's gold, Jerry, it's gold.

Well, it turns out I don't. And I didn't. That line was written by famed sports writer and novelist Dan Jenkins. For the better part of 30 years, I unknowingly and unwittingly passed it off as my own.

It was from a book I don't remember ever reading. It must have just stuck in my subconscience.

I am only mentioning it here not to apologize to Dan Jenkins. He wouldn't give a shit. But rather as a reason to give credit to Swedish writer Fredrik Backman. You might not recognize his name. He wrote a bestseller which later became a movie called *A Man Called Ove*. It is a great book. One of his other books is called *Britt-Marie Was Here*. I love the opening chapter. The main character is a prickly, opinionated curmudgeon. My type of gal. One of her lines is so good. So laugh-out-loud funny that I have adopted it into my daily lexicon. I use it often. So do some of my characters. So, while most of the words in this collection are mine, know that when you come across "are we at war" that you have Backman, not me, to thank.

Okay. Good.

Now I feel better.

THE ONE STAR REVIEW

Photograph © Gerd Altmann / pixabay.com

I feel bad for the gentiles.

Well, not all the gentiles. Just the gentile writers.

When they get a bad review, they have no one to blame but themselves.

We Jews can blame the anti semites.

Now as luck would have it, my books have been very well reviewed. *Almost the Truth* got a great review in Kirkus, a fact I manage to slip into nearly every conversation. And *Bubbe Meise* received a starred review in Blue Ink Review- where the reviewer called me an "irresistible character."

Now unless you are a writer you have likely never heard of Kirkus or Blue Ink. Most people will invariably say "is that a friend of yours?" Eventually, they will all end up asking how many books I have sold. I will then repeat "I got a great review from Kirkus" and then they will ask again how many copies I sold and I will mumble "nearly 200." Although it might be closer to 100. Then the person will sometimes say "oh, so I bought 20% of your books."

Anyway, that's what happens.

But on occasion a negative review will show up on Amazon or on Goodreads and I will show it to a friend who is always nice enough to say "antisemite." Even my non Jewish friends know to say anti semite and that makes me feel a little bit better but not really. They aren't really saying that the reviewer is antisemetic. It is just shorthand for saying you can't please everyone and I know that's true but the negative reviews really bummed me out. My friend Helen said that most writers don't read their reviews and every writer has had to suffer through bad ones. My friend Steve Levine said "at least you didn't get a Fatwah declared on you" which also made me feel better.

In the end, I decided to just go cold turkey and stop reading reviews. Instead, I ask Kitty, my admin assistant, to go through the reviews from time to time and update me on anything which is good. I tell her not to even hint at anything which might be bad. So that works pretty well although sometimes she will say that there is nothing new and I of course interpret it as being that there is nothing new which is good so by default they must be bad. Anyway it is a matter for my shrink and not my editor but it works for me.

Most people in my life now know that I am not interested in hearing about bad reviews and, if they are kind enough to write their own review, they will just forward it to me.

Of course most people in my life are not Lewberg, who has a "fuck them if they can't take a joke" attitude and doesn't understand why I don't share it, so I wasn't really surprised when he sent me a text which said

"Did you see the Amazon review from the dick who only gave you one star?"

And I replied "Jesus Lewberg."

And he said "Guy said he couldn't read the font. Said it was too small. He returned the book like it was a defective toaster. Gave you one star. That really fucks your average."

I then waited for Lewberg to text 'antisemite'. But no text came.

So I sent it myself.

"Antisemite," I texted.

And Lewberg texted back "nope."

And I said "nope?"

Lewberg texted "nope. Sheldon Levkovitch"

Then he texted "semite."

I pulled out a copy of *Almost the Truth* from my bookshelf and checked the size of the font. It was perfectly fine. Perfectly legible. Then I compared it to the one in *The Bubbe Meise*. It too was perfectly fine.

There wasn't much to do other than conclude that Sheldon Levkovitch was a myopic misanthropic piece of shit.

And there was nothing I could do about it.

Or could I?

I email our book designer and asked if she could create a file with larger print. Amazon has print on demand. In theory, we could remove the existing print file, replace it with a large print version, order a copy, and then return to the original file. It would cost me a couple of hundred of dollars in design costs, but it could be done.

It was dumb.

I should just have ignored the one star review and gotten on with my life.

But

I couldn't.

I called Lewberg and told him of my plan.

"Let me see if I got this right," he said "you are going to spend a few hundred dollars just in order to get a custom large print version of the book so you can send it to him in the hope that he will change his one star review?"

"Yes."

"Do you know who he is or where he lives?"

"No"

"Do you have any reason to think that the type of person who goes out of his way to give you a shit review because the font is too small is the type of person who will then change his review?"

"No"

"Do you even know if it is possible to change a review?"

"No."

"Of all of the bad ideas you have ever had, and you have had a few, I think this might be the worst," said Lewberg.

"It's moot unless reviews can be changed," I say.

"You won't do it just for the customer service?"

"No. Fuck him. This only makes sense if reviews and ratings can be changed. Otherwise, it is a waste of time."

"I could review your book and then see if I can change it," offered Lewberg.

"Yeah?" I said

"Sure," said Lewberg.

"It's a crazy idea," I said.

"The craziest," said Lewberg.

"Do you think it might work," I asked.

And Lewberg replied "Yeah, it just might."

Goldfarb calls me ten minutes later. He launches into the conversation without a hello.

"You still have that thing about not wanting to hear about negative reviews?"

"Goldfarb, what are you doing looking at Amazon reviews?"

"It relaxes me."

"It relaxes you?"

"Well, I thought it might be a bit cold if I said it cheered me up."

"Jesus Goldfarb!"

"What can I say. I have a thing for schadenfreude."

"No schadenfreude here Harold. You're too late. Lewberg just told me. I already heard about myopic Sheldon. I'm taking care of it."

"What are you doing?"

I told Goldfarb my plan.

"Lewberg doesn't have to test it. Of course you can edit or delete an Amazon review. I think it is a crazy waste of money but the guy might appreciate it."

Turns out though, that Sheldon Levkowitz did not really appreciate very many things. He didn't appreciate the Los Veracruz restaurant because "the paper towels in the bathroom were so coarse I feared tearing my skin." He didn't like the new James Bond movie because "I wouldn't feed that popcorn to a Guantanamo prisoner." And he didn't like Jim's Hardware store because "their parking spots appear to be only large enough for a child's tricycle." All one star reviews. This Sheldon Levkowitz was a piece of work and I realized that maybe I got off easy. So there wasn't much I could do. I would just have to live with the one star review and the drop in my overall ratings. The phone rang and it was Goldfarb.

"It's not myopic," he said.

"What's not myopic?"

"Well you called him myopic Sheldon but myopic means nearsighted. What you meant to say was hyperopic."

"Goldfarb," I said "are you fucking kidding me with this?"

"I was just thinking if you end up writing this up in one of your little stories that you are going to look pretty stupid. Some guy like Sheldon will give you one star because you got it wrong. I am only trying to help."

I thought about it. Goldfarb was probably right

"Ok thanks. If I ever write it up in one of my little stories I will fix it. Although I'm not sure I am ever going to write about this one star review."

"No not your finest moment," said Goldfarb.

"This Sheldon is quite the prolific reviewer," I said. Then I proceeded to tell Goldfarb about the other one star reviews.

And Goldfarb said "you know. I think it actually might be a good thing."

"What do you mean? This guy is just a curmudgeon."

"Yeah. But his complaints are always about secondary factors. He doesn't actually slam the product. If you fix the secondary factor, in this case, the size of the font, he might actually make a change."

"You think."

"Wouldn't hurt to try."

Kitty found a Sheldon Levkowitz in Seattle, one in Chicago, and one in Miami. We printed three copies of the book and sent one to all three Sheldons.

And then we waited.

One month.

Two months.

Three months.

Every month I asked Kitty if there was a new review from Sheldon.

Every month she said no.

On month four she sent me a very excited email. Sheldon had changed his review and had now given the book five stars.

I called Kitty

"Five stars?"

"Yes!"

"Ok. Read it to me."

"I have to compliment Amazon's commendable customer service. Upon hearing my complaint that the font on their product was too small and illegible, they replaced it with a large print version. I am impressed. Five stars."

"That's it?"

"Yes."

"Nothing about the book?"

"Let me look again... no."

"Hmm. That sucks. But five stars?"

"Yes."

"So my rating went back up."

And the phone went silent. Then Kitty said "no."

"No?"

"No."

"That's weird. Maybe it takes 24 hours for their algo to kick in. Let's check again tomorrow."

"Ok."

We checked again the next day, the day after that, and the week after too. But the rating did not go up. That didn't make sense. But I wasn't going to let it bug me.

And I didn't.

For about six hours.

At 3 am that night I turned on my computer and logged into Amazon. I found my book. Kitty was right. Sheldon had changed his review to five stars. But right below Sheldon's review was the reason why my rating did not go up.

Another 1 star review.

Which Kitty was forbidden to tell me about.

It was a review that the person who posted it was supposed to have removed. But who, perhaps with the aid of one or two Kettel Ones, had forgotten about.

This was the review.

One Star Review

"I wish that I too, like my fellow reviewer, could say that the font in this book was too small to read. Unfortunately, I was able to read it all too well. One star. Only because Amazon doesn't allow me to put in zero. Damn you Sheldon you lucky sonavabitch."

Amazon Customer Lewberg.

A SINNER'S PRAYER

Photograph © Bernabé García / pixabay.com

I don't really listen to the radio anymore. Not AM. Not FM. Not talk radio. Not sports shows. Not Howard Stern. I have XM Satellite and alternate between The Bridge, Classic Vinyl, eStreet Radio, Tom Petty, Billy Joel, and Coffee House. Sometimes a valet will switch it to a rap station and I will listen to a few songs before realizing and switching it back to something from my generation. I think my rock and roll bonafides are well-established, so I have no shame in admitting I am really okay with Christopher Cross. If I want to ride like the wind, then I will ride like the wind.

It means I don't often hear songs I don't know. But I am, quite often, reminded of old songs I haven't heard in ages. Sometimes, more often than I care to admit, old songs which I never liked the first time around which now come wrapped in a very tolerable, if not actually pleasant, nostalgic ribbon.

The exception to this musical comfort zone is The Coffee House. It is a mix of folk singers, solo singer-songwriters, and acoustic versions and covers of well-known songs. It is quite good, but you can't really listen to it for too long for fear of drifting asleep and ending up in a ditch. If you are on a road trip and want to stay awake, it is probably not a good choice. Best to revert back to Radar Love.

I do like it though and am often rewarded with a gem of an acoustic cover or the discovery of a brand new artist.

Sometimes, the song will just be so good I go home and, not only buy the song, no free downloads for me, but the entire album and, more often than not, the entire discography. That was true of songs like Liz Longley's When You've Got Trouble and Amelia Curran's The Mistress. Songs which made me sit up and pay attention. Once, driving back from a late dinner, I heard a powerful song which, for reasons I can't explain or understand, just resonated with me. Maybe it was the singer repeating the chorus of wanting to be a better man. I really don't know. But I didn't even get to listen to the entire song because it was interrupted by a phone call. When I hung up, both the song and the information about it had disappeared.

So I did something I had never done before or since. I pulled over to the side of the road and Googled some of the lyrics which were still fresh in my brain. It didn't take long.

A Sinner's Prayer.

Slaid Cleaves.

I got home and bought three of his albums. Including a live recording from the Horseshoe Lounge in Austin, which included an amazing rendition of Sinner's Prayer. The album was on constant rotation for me that summer. Although not a huge country fan, I quite liked most of the songs except for a few where he, if you can believe, yodels.

I spend my winters in Boca Raton. Turns out I am quite popular, especially with my Canadian friends and family, during those winter months, and I get my fair share of visitors. Before heading south, I check the internet to see what shows might be coming to the area. I then add them to the calendar on my phone. Then cross-reference to see if they might coincide with the schedule of my visitors.

That winter looked pretty good. Springsteen was slated for his River anniversary tour at BBT and a pair of Roger old-timers, Daltry and Hodgson, had their respective shows at Hard Rock. And, lodged somewhere in between, was a scheduled performance by the aforementioned Slaid Cleaves. On Saturday, February 24. On February 23rd, a reminder popped up on my phone. Slaid Cleaves tomorrow night. I had completely forgotten about it. I had plans with my friend Donna the next night. I texted to ask if she would be okay to go to a concert. She said sure. She didn't even ask who. She's good that way. I then called the venue to get a couple of tickets.

Sold out.

Seriously?

Yes. Weeks ago.

Okay.

I text Donna back. Forget about the concert.

She says okay.

She's good that way.

On Saturday, we agree to meet at a restaurant I don't really want to go to and see a movie I don't really want to see.

I'm not really good that way.

But I don't get to see Donna all that much, so I figure I will take one for the team.

Then at 5:00, I am not so much in the mood for taking one for the team. Also, I really want to see Slaid Cleaves. I call the venue back.

"Any chance you have a pair for Slaid Cleaves tonight?" I ask.

"A couple just cancelled. I have one pair."

"Fantastic. Let me give you my Visa number."

"Nah. Your name is fine. $30 each." I give him my name.

"I would prefer if you took my credit card info. I don't want to lose those seats."

"All good. I've got you, Mr. Levy."

"Zevy."

"What?"

"Zevy. You said Levy."

"I got you, brother."

I texted Donna. 'Change of plans. We are going to the concert. I am going down now to pick up the tickets. I will meet you at the restaurant.'

So I now speed down to Fort Lauderdale.

I have now twice used the word venue to describe where the concert is taking place. And it is, in the strictest definition of the word, a venue. But what it really is is a guitar store. That is, a store which sells guitars, banjos, amps, and other musical instruments. In a strip plaza on Commercial Blvd. I walk in two hours before the show and they are setting up. Four rows of bridge chairs in front of a stage, well no, not a stage, really just a piece of wood elevated three inches. Okay, so a stage. I pay my $60.

The guy says, "Thank you, Mr. Zevy." I think he is being a bit of a smart aleck but am too excited to notice.

Although, clearly I noticed.

I ask about seats. He says anywhere. I drape my sweatshirt so it covers two seats in the back row. The back row, just to reiterate, is the fourth row. "This okay?" Am not really understanding this. I didn't call my scalper. I didn't tip or bribe anyone. Can it really be this easy? I can just save these seats with the Whistler sweatshirt I 'borrowed' from my brother?

The guy must think I am totally whack. He nods his head. He says, "I got you, brother."

I rush Donna through dinner. No coffee. Not dessert. I am worried about my seats. About my brother's sweatshirt.

Am not comfortable in situations where I haven't slipped someone a 20.

We hurry back.

The seats and sweatshirt are where I left them (I am telling this story straight up. More or less. But I am not an idiot. I know it is much funnier if Slaid is now wearing my sweatshirt).

Donna says, "This is a guitar store!"

I say, "I know."

Donna says, "We're in the fourth row!"

I say, "I know."

Donna then whispers, pointing to a man carrying a guitar about five feet away from us, "That is Slaid Cleaves!"

I say, "Donna, yesterday you had never even heard of Slaid Cleaves."

She says, "I know. But this is pretty fucking cool!"

I say, "I know."

So Slaid Cleaves plays for us. There is another musician on bass accompanying him. They harmonize.

I don't think I need to explain the allure of an intimate concert. Donna doesn't know a single song and absolutely loved it. I know most and love it more. Slaid says he is going to take a short break and be right back. His wife has set up a table where she is selling merchandise. I line up and buy a t-shirt which has lyrics to one of his songs.

On the front it says:

My drinking days are over

On the back it says:

But I'm still trouble bound

I also buy Donna a copy of the Live at the Horseshoe Lounge CD which I already own. His wife says I can get it autographed. I'm not much of an autograph guy but decide to line up to at least meet him and shake his hand. He is very nice and I ask him if he is going to do Sinner's Prayer in the next set. He says no, he is sorry, the song isn't part of the setlist anymore. So I tell him the story about hearing the song, the phone call, pulling over to the side of the road and looking it up. "That song," I say, "is why I am here." And he says, "Let me see what I can do."

I say, "Okay, thanks."

He doesn't make me wait long. He gets back on stage and says he is going to open with a song he hadn't planned on singing. And then he tells my story. In its entirety. From that makeshift three-inch raised stage. And then he sings Sinner's Prayer.

And then Donna says, "How fucking cool is that."

And then I say, "I know, right."

We go back to the restaurant and have the coffee and dessert we missed. I give Donna the CD but I keep the t-shirt. She says she will be on the lookout for upcoming concerts. She says this was really fun.

I get into the car and realize Donna forgot to take her CD. I unwrap the covering and pop it into my player. I flip through until I get to it.

I'm not living like I should

I want to be a better man

A sinner's prayer upon my lips

A broken promise in my hand

I know that there will come a day

A heavy price I'll have to pay

I keep pretending to be good

I'm not living like I should

CORNED BEEF

Photograph © afridayinapril / pixabay.com

This story is about someone being funnier than me. Doesn't happen often. But when it does, I like to give credit, however reluctantly, where credit is due.

Although, to be fair, I'm not actually going to use his real name. But seeing as the only people who read these stories are people I know, you will all figure out who I am talking about. Which, frankly, is not all that funny for me.

Were anyone else writing this story, it would rightly be one of survival. It would be one of miracle. But that is not my story to tell. I don't write those stories. Had I been at the parting of the Red Sea, my story would have been about finding a shekel on the beach. That would have been my miracle. Or about having to walk a mile down the beach so I could find somewhere to pee in private. So if you are looking for redemption or acts of God, you've come to the wrong place. I'm just here to write this bit.

This person who is funnier than me is a childhood friend. He is an ex-roommate. We played basketball together. He still likes to call me Aaron.

In order to write this bit, I first have to talk about some unpleasant things. It is going to seem like I am glossing them over. That I don't think they are important. That is not true. But, like I said, it is not my story to tell. I am only providing a little bit of context. So here it is. My friend got the coronavirus. Was on a respirator for over two weeks. Was in a coma for more. Had a cranial bleed. Had bouts of delirium. Was unable to speak. When he could speak, it was only to spout obscenities. Then he got better. And then, as if nothing had happened, he, once again, was funnier than me.

So you can understand why I might be a little pissed off.

I mean, I'm happy he is alive and all that, but one minute he is in a coma and the next he is funnier than me.

It is a bit of a kick in the balls.

My friend has a lot of other friends. When we heard he was sick, we began a tradition of having a Zoom *l'chayim*, toast of scotch, on Friday afternoons. We would make our jokes, drink our scotch, and get updates on his condition. A couple of the guys gave us prayers to recite. I don't pray and I don't drink scotch, but every Friday, I did both. Closed my eyes, put my hand on my head to hold down an imaginary kippah, and threw my head back and downed the burning liquid. Sometimes the news was hopeful and encouraging. Other times, not as much. None of us were doctors, but those we talked to were grim.

He is on the strong respirator. He is on the regular respirator. We celebrate. He is back on the strong respirator. We Google things we don't want to Google. We tell our jokes. We drink our scotch. We say our prayers. Our friend is not 88. He does not have preexisting conditions. He is all of us. We drink our scotch. We say our prayers. We wash our hands.

And then some glimmer of hope. A friend of a friend heard of a thumbs-up. Of a laugh. Of a brief conversation. One of the boys is in charge of giving us updates. But those updates are not enough. It is a small community. It is a tight community. "I heard from a friend of his wife," says one. "My sister is a good friend of his brother," says another. "Have you heard? Any news?" And then more progress. "You heard he was sitting up and made a joke?" I text it to 20 people. Then to 20 more. One day, one of the boys emails the group and says, "Guess who I just spoke to." That was on my birthday. Best present ever! Then another gets a call. A message left at his office. He can't get over it. "How the fuck does he remember my office number?"

Then we all had our turns. He sounded good. Sounded strong. Funny, even. I told him I had had chest pains while running this past winter. Thought I might have angina. But the nuclear test gave me the all-clear. The cardiologist said it was more likely I die of gonorrhea.

My friend said, "Let me get this straight. Are you trying to one-up me? I was dead twice."

Okay. Funny.

But funnier than me?

C'mon. Let's be serious.

I ask my brother if he has spoken to our friend. He said he tried him but he didn't pick up. "Let me try him again." He calls and puts it on speaker. Our friend picks up on the first ring. My brother says, "Where the hell have you been? I have been trying you all day." Our friend says, "Sorry, buddy, you have to catch me between my sponge baths."

Fuck.

That was funny.

And then my brother says our next Zoom will have a special guest. But his camera is taking a little time to work, so we only have audio. I say, "We don't need to see his face, because we can look at Brian in order to see someone who looks like he just got out of a coma."

That gets a good laugh.

Then the camera kicks in and there is our friend. He is wearing a Raptors hat. They have shaven his two-month beard so we miss seeing his Grizzly Adams look. He has lost a few pounds, but when he stands, he still looks like a former six-foot-two basketball player.

Everyone is doing material. We are all fighting for attention.

Someone makes the mistake of saying he looks and sounds the same as before. The rest of us quickly and unapologetically make it clear we don't necessarily think that's a good thing. We are 13 again. The jokes haven't improved. But they are our jokes.

Then someone asks if he is back on real food. My friend says yes. He says he is craving a corned beef sandwich. Could someone drive downtown to the rehab center and sneak one in?

"First guy to bring me a corned beef sandwich," says my friend, who recovered from COVID, who was on a respirator, who was in a coma, who had a cranial bleed, who couldn't speak, "First guy who brings me a corned beef sandwich gets a year's worth of my antibodies."

Now that is funny.

Funnier than me.

So welcome back, my friend.

But fuck you.

Fuck you and the horse you rode in on.

CARL THE COYOTE

This is Carl.

Carl the Coyote.

Carl the Coyote is a rubber decoy my brother asked me to order from Amazon.

Because of the geese.

And their shit.

My brother was tired of stepping on and cleaning geese shit on the dock. He was tired of people walking into the house with goose-shit-laden shoes. He was tired of constantly asking everyone if they were wearing their inside shoes.

He was tired of the geese.

The geese were his great white whale.

Carl was now his third attempt to thwart the geese and their respective shit. The first had been putting up a wire fence around the perimeter. He had sent me to Home Depot to buy the fence. He had spent time sitting on the deck observing their formation and taking notes on the trajectory path of their advance team. He had identified and pinpointed the area of entry on the beachfront.

Normandy in Muskoka.

I should probably mention at this point that should you encounter my brother and he should then launch into a long diatribe about geese and his ongoing battles with them, then it is probably not a good idea to say, "It's only shit." He doesn't take kindly to that.

We put up the fence and in the morning woke to find a blanket of geese feces on the lawn and on the dock. Perhaps they, too, had gone to Home Depot and acquired wire cutters or perhaps their engineering corps had constructed a makeshift bridge. Or perhaps, as I have previously suggested, it was as simple as the notion that geese could fly.

Nevertheless, it was clear the fence did not work and it was time to go to Plan B.

Plan B was a motion-detector sprinkler system which generated a spray of cold water. I have to be honest, I was very skeptical at first. It sounded a little too good to be true. But it turned out the sprinkler system was something of an engineering and mechanical marvel: any time any member of the Zevy family walked within 20 yards of the sprinkler, we would get sprayed. The geese however, got away scot-free.

"Can you please turn off the fucking sprinkler" soon replaced "are those your indoor shoes" as the most used phrase in our family.

Then my sister-in-law made the mistake of saying, "It's only shit." Dinner that night was very, very quiet.

My brother, his head buried in the virtual cloud, was undeterred.

"They may have won the battle, but they will not win the war," he declared.

He scoured the cottage owner message boards. One thing kept coming up over and over: coyotes.

And so we bought Carl.

My brother and the geese signed an armistice at dawn. It was a very moving ceremony.

For seven days, we encountered neither geese nor their shit.

Hail to Carl.

With my brother now in a perfectly jovial mood, I thought it might be a good time to ask if I could invite a guest to the cottage.

Amelia Reynolds.

Now ordinarily I don't need permission to invite a guest to the cottage, because I have my own little bunkie on the property and my family are only too happy to see what kind of deranged woman would agree to spend a weekend in that tiny bunkie. The problem however was this woman and I had not reached the point in our nascent relationship where sleeping anywhere near me nor my bunkie was a possibility. In fact, inviting her to the cottage, to swim in the refreshing lake waters while the city experienced a record heat wave, was my attempt to change the parameters of the aforementioned fledgling relationship.

So I needed them to agree to let her stay in the main cottage.

Amelia Reynolds was dying to come to the cottage.

Now neither Amelia Reynolds nor I was crass enough, well Amelia Reynolds certainly wasn't, to suggest or admit that a weekend at the cottage meant a symbolic fast-forward button had been pressed, but, at the very least, it would be a sign of progress.

My brother agreed at once and my sister-in-law, now virtually ebullient about not getting sprayed by the sprinkler every time she went to the dock and now able to wear her outside shoes wherever the fuck she wanted, also was on board.

"I think it is a little weird," she said. "But she is welcome to stay in the Moose Room."

Three times on the drive up, Amelia Reynolds asked if there would be a bonfire and if we could make s'mores. I assured her there was and we could. I even sent my brother to the grocery store to get extra graham crackers and marshmallows.

Dinner was fantastic. My brother and sister-in-law put on a great spread. Rib eye, salad, baked potato. My brother even made his famous beefsteak tomato and parmesan cheese appetizer. The wine was flowing and my nieces were charming and doting. Not once did anyone throw me under the bus.

We decided to eat the key lime pie along with s'mores at the dock. My brother and nieces went down first in order to build the bonfire while Amelia Reynolds and I cleaned up and loaded the dishwasher.

Not once did my sister-in-law say, although she was surely thinking it, that this was the first time I loaded the dishwasher all summer.

The night was going perfectly. It was magical.

"Let's go down," I said. But Amelia Reynolds said she wanted to take a quick shower and change into her sweats. She said she would be super fast. That I would be very impressed. Then Amelia Reynolds kissed me.

Amelia Reynolds was true to her word. Her shower was super fast. It was already dark, but my family had built a huge bonfire and it was casting a pretty strong light. It wasn't that far from the cottage to the dock.

We had had Carl for only a week. During that time, I had been startled twice and my sister-in-law and each of my nieces once. And we knew he was there.

Carl was a rubber decoy, but he was pretty convincing.

Amelia Reynolds did not know about Carl.

That was my bad. That's on me.

It was hard to believe anyone could scream that loudly.

Amelia Reynolds screamed very, very loudly.

For a very long time.

We finally calmed her down and showed her that Carl wasn't real.

Amelia Reynolds was now in a state. She thought it was a prank. She thought we had set her up with a practical joke. It wasn't clear if she was angry, horrified, or just plain embarrassed. Either way, she said she wanted to go home.

My brother, my sister-in-law, and nieces all tried to explain about the geese. About the shit. But Amelia Reynolds would not be placated. She went to the Moose Room, packed her bags and got into my car. I begged her to stay. "At least wait until morning," I said. But Amelia Reynolds said she didn't want to spend another minute at the cottage.

So I drove her home.

She calmed down on the drive home and I thought we had smoothed things over. But I never saw Amelia Reynolds again.

My brother texted me a picture the next morning. Actually, he sent it to the family group chat. Here is the picture. With it he included a caption.

'Carl having tea with the geese.'

Yup. If you look closely, you can see Carl surrounded by a flock of geese.

Then Danna texted what everyone else was thinking.

'I guess Carl only works on Uncle Ronnie's dates. 😀'

THE BUBBE MEISE

Photograph © Wikimedia Commons

My friend Ruthie texted me. 'Avital Kaplan had twins.' Avital Kaplan was the daughter of one of our old friends from Ottawa.

I texted back, 'Mazel tov!!'

I don't know why people are compelled to tell me these things. But they do. And now my friend Golda was going to call me from Israel and tell me the Avraham Kashitsky story again. Every time someone had a multiple birth, she would call and tell me the Avraham Kashitsky story. She loved that story.

I don't blame her.

It's a great story.

Only, it wasn't true.

'Gotta go, Ruthie,' I texted. 'Golda is about to call.'

'How do you know?' she asked.

'Because I know.' Just then the phone rang. It was Golda.

"You heard about Avital Kaplan?"

I said, "Yes. Mazel tov, mazel tov."

"Soon by you," said Golda. Am not sure why she was hoping I impregnate someone at this stage of my life, but I said what I always said:

"Thank you."

Golda did not waste time.

"Twins," she said. "*Baruch hashem*. It makes me think of Avraham Kashitsky."

"Golda," I said gently. "That story is not true. It is a '*bubbe meise*.' An old wives' tale."

"Of course it's true! We know him. It is '*emes*.' It is a true story. It is a beautiful story."

"You know him?"

"Of course!"

"Tell me again how you know him."

We had had this conversation a dozen times. But it didn't stop Golda from telling me again.

"You know the Kornblatts next door?"

I knew the Kornblatts.

Golda wasn't waiting for my response.

"Reuben is our next-door neighbour. He has a cousin who lives in Crown Heights."

"His cousin is Avraham Kashitsky?" I knew the cousin wasn't Avraham Kashitsky. I was just egging Golda on.

"No, the cousin got married. His best man was Nachum Kashitsky. Avraham Kashitsky is Nachum Kashitsky's brother."

"Okay. So Avraham Kashitsky is Reuben Kornblatt's cousin's best man's brother?"

"Yes." Golda did not think for one second that it was a bit of a stretch. "I don't understand why you don't believe the story."

"I do believe the story," I said. "I just don't believe it is true."

"You're impossible," said Golda.

"The story is apocryphal," I said. But she had already hung up.

Now here's the thing about the Avraham Kashitsky story. Even though I didn't believe it for a second, I actually told it all the time. Because, you know, it's a good story.

The more I told it, the more people told me they had heard the story themselves. My friends Donnie and Beth said their accountant went to grad school with a woman who knew Avraham Kashitsky's wife. My niece Rachel's boyfriend Daniel said he heard Lebron James had told the story in the Cavalier locker room. It was ridiculous. The story was completely made up. And I would have continued to believe it was a bubble meise if my friend Solly's appendix had not burst.

Lewberg, Goldfarb and Lewberg's friend Solly had decided to go on a once-in-a-lifetime golf trip to Pebble Beach. Pebble Beach was also on my bucket list, but they had chosen to go in February and I refused to fly across the country for three days of freezing weather, rain, and howling winds.

Also, Goldfarb was a bit of a mope.

But then Solly's appendix burst and the flight, hotel, and rounds were prepaid and non-refundable, so I decided to bite the bullet.

But the weather, shockingly, proved to be perfect. There was a slight breeze coming in from the ocean. The views were breathtaking.

It was a stroke of good luck and we should all have been thrilled.

But Lewberg, true to form, was bitter.

The Pebble Beach bar did not stock Ketel One.

"Absolut," he said as he poured his usual splash of cranberry. "$500 a round and they have Absolut."

We both knew after three drinks the brand would not matter. But it was all about principle for Lewberg.

"Are we at war?"

Goldfarb was also a little bitter. He didn't like playing with strangers. The starter had asked us if we would mind if a fourth joined us. Of course we would mind! But none of us had the guts to say it. Pebble Beach rounds were notoriously slow. Now we would have to spend the next five hours with a complete stranger. He would be in our group pictures.

The starter pointed him out. He was hitting balls on the range. He had a nice swing. "C'mon," I said. "Let's go introduce ourselves."

Both Goldfarb and Lewberg looked like they were about to cry.

The fourth saw us walking towards him and he stopped his practice and turned to greet us. We all took off our caps, as golfers do, shook hands and made introductions.

"Avraham Kashitsky," he said with a grin. "I appreciate you guys letting me tag along. My partner cancelled at the last minute."

I said, "Did you say Avraham Kashitsky?"

He said, "Yes."

"You're not from Cleveland by any chance?"

"I am, as a matter of fact. From Shaker Heights. Do we know each other?"

I said, "No, but I have been waiting to meet you for 25 years."

Goldfarb was thrilled I volunteered to ride in a cart with Avraham Kashitsky. After we all hit our tee shots on number one, I turned to Avraham Kashitsky and said, "I tell an Avraham Kashitsky story." He said, "You tell an Avraham Kashitsky story?" I said, "Yeah."

He said, "What Avraham Kashitsky do you tell?" I said, "I tell the 770 Parkway Story." Avraham Kashitsky said, "That's funny, I tell the 770 Parkway Story too." So I said, "Why don't you tell me your version and I'll tell you how it compares to my story?"

So Avraham Kashitsky began to tell me his Avraham Kashitsky 770 Parkway Story. I had waited all my life to play Pebble Beach.

But I had waited even longer to hear the Avraham Kashitsky 770 Parkway story.

This is the story he told. It was, to a word, the exact same story I told.

Avraham Kashitsky and his wife desperately wanted to have a baby. But they had no luck. They tried all the medical options and procedures but to no avail. Avraham Kashitsky's brother Nachum said that the best man at his wedding, who was Reuben Kornblatt's first cousin, suggested he go get a blessing from the Lubavitcher Rebbe in Brooklyn. Avraham Kashitsky said he didn't really think a blessing from the Lubavitcher Rebbe was going to help. His brother Nachum responded in the quintessential Jewish manner.

He said, "It couldn't hurt."

So Avraham Kashitsky and his wife travelled from Shaker Heights, Ohio, to 770 Eastern Parkway in Brooklyn which was the headquarters of Chabad Lubavitch. They stood in line in the hot sun for five hours waiting for a 10-second audience and blessing from the Rebbe.

The Rebbe had a tradition of handing out crisp one-dollar bills to everyone who stood in line. The recipient would then give the dollar to charity.

I told Avraham Kashitsky that I was not a religious man but I was a huge fan of the tenet that the meeting of two men should benefit a third.

When Avraham Kashitsky and his wife finally got to the front of the line, they told the Rebbe they were trying to have a baby and wanted his blessing.

The Lubavitcher Rebbe gives everyone a crisp one-dollar bill.

But he did not give Avraham Kashitsky and his wife a crisp dollar bill.

He gave them three.

I said to Avraham Kashitsky, "Are you fucking with me?"

And Avraham Kashitsky said, "My hand to God."

The number seven hole at Pebble Beach is the signature par three. It is generally considered the most famous par three hole in the world. It is very short, downhill, with the Pacific Ocean in the background.

The hole was only playing 122 yards that day. It was downhill and there wasn't much of a breeze. Lewberg and Avraham Kashitsky were longer hitters than Goldfarb and I, and they both hit a sand wedge. Goldfarb hit a pitching wedge. All three hit the green. Lewberg said four balls on the green would make a great picture.

"No pressure or anything," I joked. I then took out a gap wedge. I hit it pure. I hit it very high. It landed on the green, took two bounces and plunked right into the hole.

It was my first-ever hole in one.

At Pebble Beach.

On the iconic number seven.

Nobody said anything for a second. I think we were all in shock. Then Lewberg said:

"Fucking Zakarian!"

And then Goldfarb said:

"Fucking Zakarian!"

Then I said:

"Fucking Zakarian."

Avraham Kashitsky, who had no idea what we were talking about, who had no way of knowing that Zakarian was a golfer at our Florida country club who dropped dead of a heart attack after making a hole in one, gave me a high five and then said:

"Fucking Zakarian."

Not going to lie. I texted or emailed everyone I knew. Plus a lot of people I didn't know. We took a nice picture of the four of us standing next to the pin with me holding the ball. I had no shame. I sent everyone that picture.

My friend Golda doesn't really understand golf, but she knew a hole in one was a big deal. She texted me a mazel tov. She recognized Lewberg and Goldfarb, they were two of my oldest friends, but she wanted to know who the other guy was.

I said it was Avraham Kashitsky.

This story has a great kicker. It is coming up. But my favorite part is not the kicker. It is what Golda said next.

She didn't say, 'No fucking way.' We had both been telling the Avraham Kashitsky story for 25 years, but she was totally nonplussed he was in my hole-in-one picture.

She didn't say, 'Omg that is unbelievable!'

Instead she said:

'He's taller than I thought.'

I fucking love that line!

I texted, 'Hold on, I am going to send you another picture.'

I did.

It was a picture that Avraham Kashitsky had emailed me after the round.

Of his triplets.

Three crisp one-dollar bills.

Then Golda said, "Bubbe meise my ass."

No, she didn't really.

She's not like that.

PACKAGE FROM AMAZON

Lewberg tells me I look like shit.

I say, "More than usual?"

He says, "Yeah, more than usual."

I say, "I haven't been sleeping. I am up every two hours to pee."

He says, "Every two hours?"

I say, "You can set your watch to it."

He says, "Well, you can do one of two things."

And I say, "Okay, what?"

"Well, you can drag your bed into the bathroom. Or you can go see a urologist."

Lewberg isn't joking. I tell him I think I will go see a urologist.

Lewberg says, "Think I have a guy."

Lewberg's guy is a tiny shell of a man, Dr. Patel, who can hit the ball a mile. I know he can hit the ball a mile because my appointment is on the golf course. Lewberg has invited him as a guest to our golf club. He says he has played here before. With a former patient of his. Some Armenian chap. Dr. Patel speaks with a pronounced English accent. Lewberg and I can't envision Zakarian ever bringing a guest, but perhaps he made an exception for the man who gave him his yearly prostate exam.

For seven holes, all we talk about is golf. On the tee on number eight, he turns to me and says:

"Every two hours?"

And I say, "Yeah."

And he says, "How much urine are we talking about?"

And I say, "I don't know."

And he says, "Find out. Then get back to me." Then he hits a six iron to within 10 feet of the pin.

When I get back from golf, I go on Amazon to order what I need. While I am there, I see it says that the iPad I ordered a few days before has been delivered. I go check my front porch but it isn't there. Then I take a look in front of the garage and it isn't there either. I go back to Amazon using the old iPad I had planned to replace and click on 'Track Your Package.' It says it was delivered at 4:00. It even has a picture of the package lying on the porch next to the front door. I click on the picture. I can see the package clearly.

Only, that isn't my front door.

I walk outside with the iPad, trying to match the front door with a front door of one of my neighbour's. But the WiFi isn't strong enough, so I go back to the house, get my iPhone, and log back into Amazon and pull up the picture.

I walk up the street and find the door.

And my package.

It is three doors down.

I should really just walk up to the porch and grab my package but I don't want anyone to think I am stealing a package, even though it is my own package, so instead I ring the bell. A woman who I have never ever seen before, a woman who lives three doors down, comes out and I explain my package situation.

She nods her head and then says, "You're the Canadian guy who lives three doors down?"

I say, "Yes."

"Are you single?"

I am now kicking myself about having done the right thing.

I say, "Yes."

She says, "I have a niece. Come in. I will show you a picture." She insisted I call her right away and so, sitting on the couch in the living room, with my Amazon package in one hand and my neighbour's phone in the other, I made a date with her niece for the following Wednesday.

To be perfectly honest, she was better looking than her picture. Much better looking than her picture. In the history of blind dates, when has that ever happened? She lived up in Fort Lauderdale and we were going to a play in Delray, and, since I was on the way, she offered to pick me up. I opened the door and there she stood, wearing a yellow sundress, smelling of lilacs, and holding a small Amazon box in her hands.

"I come bearing gifts," she said with a smile, and I liked her immediately.

I invited her in and asked if she wanted a glass of wine. We had a little time before going to the theatre.

She said sure and I then asked red or white. She said she would happily drink whatever I had open. I went to the fridge and took out a bottle of Chardonnay I had been chilling in the fridge.

As I struggled with the corkscrew, she called out from the living room, "Shall we see what I brought you?"

I walked back to the living room, a glass in each hand. "Sorry?"

She relieved me of a glass and pointed to the box. "Can we see what you ordered?"

I liked her comfort and confidence. And like I said, she looked better than her picture.

"Have at it," I said.

Now you have to understand I ordered and received packages from Amazon all the time. A week rarely went by without the appearance of a box or two. I ordered often and impulsively. I say this in my defence, because I really had no idea what was in the box.

She tore into it like a five year old on Christmas morning, finally holding aloft the prize: three plastic measuring cups. Each a different size, with red demarcation lines, some colored more boldly than others, and numbers on the side.

"Baking a cake?" she said with a smile.

Measuring cups. I had completely forgotten I had ordered them.

You have to understand I am a very good liar. I also pride myself at being quick-witted and fast on my feet. And this was an easy one. I could have come up with a dozen plausible reasons why I had ordered these measuring cups. So I am not really sure why I defaulted to the truth. Maybe it was the sundress. Maybe it was the lilacs. Maybe I just didn't want to start this relationship with a fabrication. Either way, the words which then spewed from my mouth had probably not been used at the beginning of a blind date before.

"No," I replied with a terse smile of my own. "I am using them to measure my nightly urine production."

THE WOMAN IN THE CAFE

Photograph © Alberto Bogo / Stocksy.com

The woman in the cafe was reading my book. She was a tall elegant woman with a black shawl wrapped around her shoulder. She was not wearing sunglasses, because she had removed them to read my book, but she had a pair of those big oversized sunglasses which Princess Grace of Monaco and Jackie Onassis used to wear. She was dipping her croissant into her cafe au lait like the French do. She did look French, but I was hoping she were Swiss. I'm not sure why. We were more than the required six feet away, but I could see she was reading the third edition, the one with the green cover, and I was pleased about that, because it was the best edition and had almost no typos.

It was a nice scene. One I had envisioned many times. A cultured woman of letters taking a mid-morning break from high-brow literature and philanthropic activities to snack on my little

185

vignettes together with her coffee and croissant. I soaked it in along with the sunshine which was warming this late fall day.

I craned my neck a little to see how much she had read and whether I could determine which story she had landed upon. She hadn't laughed or smiled yet, which was understandable because not all of the stories were humorous.

But still.

She must have felt my gaze, I guess I had been staring for quite a long time, because she looked up, put the book down and addressed me directly.

"Can I help you?" she said as she put on her glasses. It wasn't a waitress taking your order 'can I help you?' It was a step-off-creep 'can I help you?' which I frankly found to be a little harsh.

Also, she was neither French nor Swiss. Her voice was Toronto through and through.

I quickly apologized and explained I was just noticing the book she was reading. Was she enjoying it?

Just then an itinerant cloud blocked the sun and I felt a sudden chill.

Just as she said, "Not so much. A friend bought it for me and said I might like it, but I don't know what she was thinking."

Okay then.

Well, that was that.

"Okay," I said, "Sorry to have troubled you. Have a nice day."

Which should have ended this ephemeral conversation, but then she decided to add, "Thanks. This book is not helping." Then she took off her glasses, put them down on the table, and resumed reading the book.

My book.

The sky was really clouding up. Looked like we might even get some rain.

Well, not everyone was going to like the book. It was what it was.

But, of course, I could not let it go.

I said, "I'm terribly sorry to bother you again, but if the book is so bad, why are you still reading it?"

She put down the book, put her glasses back on and said, "Not that it's any of your business, but I am the type of person who finishes a book no matter how bad it is."

And I said, "Okay."

But she wasn't done. "Also, I have nothing else to read, so if I didn't have this book, I might end up bothering people at nearby tables like you are doing."

Well, I was now truly chastened and put in my place.

So I said, "Actually, I wrote it. That is my book."

I said it just to make her feel bad. I'm not proud of it.

She flipped the book around and examined the author picture, put on her sunglasses, I guess they might have been prescription, and looked at me, took off her sunglasses, examined the author picture again, put her sunglasses back on and said:

"You don't look as good as in your picture. You kinda need a haircut."

So much about making her feel bad.

"What don't you like about the book?" I was now clearly a glutton for punishment.

She said, "You really want to know?"

And I said, "Yes." Although I really didn't.

She said, "Look, it's not like you are a bad writer. It's just you don't know what you want to be. Are you writing fiction? Are you writing memoirs? Just make up your mind and pick one thing."

"I blur the line between fact and fiction," I said, quoting one of my reviews.

"It is confusing," she said, "and actually pretty annoying. Friends appearing in your fiction and fictitious characters in your memoirs. It is all a little too much. Sorry. But you asked."

"Okay," I said, "I think that's fair."

"Okay," she replied. "You seem very nice. I didn't mean to hurt your feelings."

"Quite okay," I said. "No harm done. Besides, I think I am going to write you out of this story."

And she said, "You're what?"

I said, "Well, this story really isn't going where I had hoped. I think I am just going to write you out of it."

"You are going to write me out of it?"

I said, "Yeah. This is one of those stories when a fictitious character appears in my real life. It is made up. I really didn't meet a woman in a cafe reading a book."

"But you did."

"Not so much. I made the whole thing up."

"Aren't we like halfway through the story?"

"Will give it a quick edit. Happens all the time."

"Well," she said with a huff, "it all seems a little capricious."

"Pretty big word for a fictitious character," I said.

She angrily returned to her book. I ordered a croissant of my own from the waitress who had sweetly said, "Can I help you?"

Okay. So it was petty. I admit it. But she pushed my buttons. I could write in a much more sympathetic character. Easily. What did I need that aggravation for?

We sat there in silence for about five minutes. We were both stewing.

Then she looked up and said, "Your mother's eulogy was quite sweet."

I said, "Thanks."

"And that mattress story was pretty funny."

I said, "Thanks."

"And all the Egypt stuff was quite interesting. I didn't mind that."

I said, "Thanks. So maybe not that bad?"

She said, "Maybe."

We sat in silence for a few more minutes. Then she said, "I know it is now moot, but how did you describe me?"

"How did I describe you?"

"Yes."

I scrolled up.

"Hmm. Here it is. Tall and elegant."

"Tall and elegant?"

"Yes."

"You make me sound matronly."

"Oh no. It wasn't my intention."

"You could have said beautiful. It wouldn't have killed you to say beautiful."

I was now a little dumbstruck. Things had started moving in the right direction, but now they were taking a turn for the worse.

"Well," I stuttered, "you were quite far away. And you were wearing your sunglasses." I knew the minute I said it that it was both a lie and a mistake.

"My sunglasses? My sunglasses? I wasn't wearing my sunglasses. You weren't paying attention to me. You were only interested in your precious book!"

"Well I—well I—" I stammered. But it was too late. She left some change on the table and stormed off.

Well. That was a shame.

I finished the rest of my croissant and left.

I was right about the rain. It started just as I left the cafe. It wasn't a long walk home, but I didn't want to get drenched, so I put on my mask and jumped on the downtown bus.

The woman in the seat in front of me was reading my book.

It was the first edition. The one with all of the typos.

But still.

You never know.

I scrolled back up a few sentences and made the change.

There was a really beautiful woman in the seat in front of me reading my book.

SHPRINTZA

I met Siobhán Rooney on an Air Canada flight from Toronto to Tel Aviv in the summer of 1980. I was 21, had recently graduated with a useless degree in political science, and had absolutely no idea what I wanted to do with my life. I figured a trip to Israel would be something I could do in the meantime. Siobhán, in a sense, was in the same boat. She had also just graduated, from Tufts in her hometown of Boston. Flying from Toronto proved to be cheaper than New York.

We spoke for about an hour before exchanging names. She had a pretty thick Boston accent. The 'Southie' brogue which Matt Damon and Ben Affleck later showcased in Good Will Hunting. Am a little embarrassed to say I tried to show off.

"Ah Siobhán," I said, "the name which does not sound like it is spelled."

"My cross to bear," she said with a smile. *"And it's not even my first name. It is my middle name. My given name is even more difficult."*

"Wow, your parents really went to town."

"You have no idea."

"Ok, go ahead and hit me. I can't wait to hear it."

"I could tell you but then I would have to kill you," she laughed.

"Fair enough. I can wait."

But I didn't have to wait long. Two minutes later the stewardess was in our aisle with our in-flight meals. What she then said gave birth to this story.

"I have a kosher meal for a Shprintza Rooney."

"That's me," said Siobhán.

I looked at her. I guess gaped at her would be a better description.

"Irish Catholic," she said with a shrug. *"But I heard the kosher meals were better. For once I can take advantage of my given name."*

"Shprintza? Your given name is Shprintza."

"Yup."

"Go on," I said.

"It's a long story," she said.

"Well," I said, peeling back the cover of my non-kosher roast chicken which did not look nearly as good as her schnitzel, *"I'm not going anywhere."*

This is the story she told me.

****

Boston, 1960

"Over my dead body," Miriam declared, as she ladled the chicken soup into a bowl.

"A thousand dollars is a lot of money," replied Reuben. "We could use the money."

"Have you lost your mind, Reuben? Shprintza?!?! We are going to call our first born Shprintza?"

"It's just a name. A name doesn't define who you are or who you will be. Can I have another matzo ball?"

"I don't want to hear another word about it. Throw that newspaper out. What kind of crazy person takes an ad out like that? Mary Elizabeth dear," she said, addressing the also-pregnant woman who was scrubbing a pot. "Just soak it overnight. It will be much easier to clean in the morning."

Miriam's mother-in-law paid for the cleaning lady. A favor she never forgot to remind her of.

"Yes, ma'am," Mary Elizabeth said, only too happy to stop scrubbing and get off her feet.

"Just take the trash out and head on home. Your feet must be killing you. Reuben! Reuben! Give Mary Elizabeth the newspaper to throw into the trash."

Mary Elizabeth took the trash and grabbed the newspaper. The trash she threw into the big grey garbage bin. But the newspaper, the Jewish Advocate, the newspaper she put into her purse.

****

"Read it again," Billy said, as he turned down Gunsmoke.

Mary Elizabeth put on her reading glasses and opened the newspaper to the notice on the second to last page which she'd circled and highlighted in yellow. *"I will pay a $1000 honorarium if you name your first-born daughter after my late grandmother Shprintza Nachama Goldberg of blessed memory who perished in Auschwitz. Only serious applicants need apply.* There's a Boston phone number."

"Crazy lady," snorted Billy.

"A thousand dollars is a lot of money," Mary Elizabeth said.

"Darling, no Jewish woman is going to give a Catholic $1000 to name her baby Shpinger."

"Shprintza. I looked it up. It means hope."

"Mary Elizabeth Rooney. You don't think it's hard enough growing up poor in south Boston, and now you want to saddle your daughter with some crazy name of some dead old lady?"

"It means hope. I kinda like it. We would be honoring her memory. Maybe bring us and her some good luck."

"That first Shprintza," he said, "sounds like she had no good luck at all."

"$1000. That's free money. She is already bringing us good luck. I am going to call in the morning."

"Mary Elizabeth. If that crazy Jewish lady hands you $1000 to give your daughter the name of her dead grandmother then you can go ahead and call me Moses because our house is nothing but a house of miracles. Now come over here and I'll rub your feet."

****

"I'm Janice. On the phone you said your name was Mary Elizabeth Rooney. Is it Mary Elizabeth or just Mary?"

"I wish it were just Mary. But it has been Mary Elizabeth all my life. It is my cross to bear for being Irish."

"I get it," Janice said with a smile.

"Irish Catholic ma'am. Janice. On both sides. On all sides. I didn't know if that would be a problem."

"It's not," said Janice, "we are all god's children. And being a redhead is a bonus."

"Well it's about time that worked to my advantage."

"Well come on in. Where did you hear about my situation?"

"In the Jewish advocate. I work for a Jewish family. I can even make a challah." Mary Elizabeth did not know why she had said that. She was a little bit nervous.

"Well I would love to try it. Maybe you can even give me a baking lesson. Can I make you a coffee?"

"Yes please. Cream and sugar please."

"When are you due?"

"Four weeks. But if the good Lord said today, he wouldn't get any argument from me. You never had kids?"

"I wasn't able to. Probably a good thing. My husband would have left me if I had called our daughter Shprintza. Although he did leave me. But for completely different reasons."

"I'm sorry, ma'am."

"Don't be, Mary Elizabeth. Tell me, what were you thinking of calling your daughter before this?"

"Well Billy, he's my husband. Billy is partial to Dorothy. It was his mother's name. We would call her Dot."

"Dot Rooney. That's nice. A whole lot nicer than Shprintza Rooney," she said smiling. "I mean, I understand why everyone is saying no. It's quite a mouthful. But $1000 is all I can afford."

"Well at least Shprintza is only one name. I have been Mary Elizabeth my whole life."

"You might be right," replied Janice Goldberg. "Here, let me show you a picture," she said as she handed Mary Elizabeth a creased 3 by 5 black and white photo.

It was a family portrait. It looked like it may have been taken by an actual photographer.

"Here," Janice pointed to a pigtailed ragamuffin kneeling in the front. "That was Shprintza. They said she was a real troublemaker."

"What's that next to her feet?" asked Mary Elizabeth.

Janice chuckled. "That's her pet chicken Haman. My Uncle Rachum said that chicken followed her everywhere."

"You see the boy standing tall in the back? That's Rachum. My uncle. He and my mother are the only ones in the picture who survived the camps. Everyone else perished."

"My lord," said Mary Elizabeth.

Just then the phone trilled.

"Will you excuse me?"

"Yes, of course." Mary Elizabeth examined the photo. It was too horrible to even imagine.

When Janice Goldberg came back, she had a pained expression on her face.

"I am so sorry, Mary Elizabeth."

"That call was from a family in Boro Park. You know, in Brooklyn?"

Mary Elizabeth did not know Boro Park.

"Anyway, they are very orthodox. And very poor. They were thrilled to get the $1000. And although it isn't their firstborn daughter - it will be their ninth kid - they are very comfortable with the name. It isn't even that uncommon in the orthodox community. So, my grandmother's memory will be honored. I am so sorry."

Nine kids. Oh my Lord. "Thanks for letting me know, Miss Goldberg... Janice. I am real happy for you."

Janice Goldberg pressed a $100 bill onto Mary Elizabeth's hand. "Here, Mary Elizabeth. Please take this."

"Oh no, Mrs. Goldberg. I'll be alright."

"For the baby. For Dot. You can buy her a nice crib. Please. It will make me feel better."

"Okay, Janice. Thank you kindly. I will buy a crib. For Dot. Much appreciated."

Then Mary Elizabeth got her coat, closed the door, and took the bus back home.

****

"$100?" said Billy.

"She just went and gave you $100?"

"Yes, she was nice. She told me all about her grandmother. Well, the little she knew. She was from a small little village in Poland. Was very poor. Barely had enough food to eat."

And then she whispered, not loud enough for Billy to hear, "And she also had a pet chicken."

"Sounds like us," said Billy with a laugh. "We are from a small village in Boston. C'mon now. Let's watch some TV."

****

Mary Elizabeth loved to take Dot out for long walks. She proudly pushed her stroller through the streets of Boston every day. Dot was a beautiful baby and a day rarely went by without a flurry of oohs and ahs from fellow Bostonian denizens. Sometimes she liked to get on the bus with her stroller and baby and go for walks in the leafy gentrified neighborhoods many blocks from her home.

So it was just by chance, one unseasonably warm April afternoon, that she found herself right in front of Janice Goldberg's townhouse just as she was walking out the door.

"Mary Elizabeth Rooney! I can't believe it! And oh my goodness, is this Dot? She's an angel."

"Yes, Mrs. Goldberg. Dorothy Molly Rooney. But we call her Dot. She is my bundle of joy."

"Now Mary Elizabeth. You call me Janice. Can I hold her?"

"Of course you can, Janice. And we just love the crib. Don't we, Dot?"

Janice Goldberg held the baby in her arms. "Well this just makes my day."

Mary Elizabeth proudly watched Janice Goldberg coo over her baby. She could tell she was a good woman. "Janice?" She asked. "How are things over in Brooklyn? In... Boro Park. How is baby Shprintza?"

Janice handed Dot back to Mary Elizabeth.

"Well you'll never believe it," she said with a smile. "It was a boy. The doctors were sure she was having a girl, but boy oh boy did they get it wrong. So Shprintza is now Shmuel. They sent me a picture. A beautiful boy. But not as beautiful as Dot."

"Oh, Janice, I'm so sorry."

"Oh, don't be. Can never be sorry about a healthy baby. Two healthy babies. They wanted to give me back the money, but I insisted they keep it. I think my grandmother, may she rest in peace, would have understood."

"Am sure she would," said Mary Elizabeth.

"Will you come in for a coffee or maybe something stronger?" Said Janice.

"Another time," said Mary Elizabeth. "But I can't have anything stronger," she smiled and rubbed her belly, "because I am pregnant."

****

"So let me get this straight," I said. "You get Shprintza Siobhán and your sister gets Dot?"

"Yup, classic middle child syndrome," she says.

"There is another?"

"Another girl. Elizabeth Mary."

"But that's..."

"The reverse of my mother's name."

"Wow. They really did a number on you."

"It's not so bad. Shprintza is only my legal name. On my passport and birth certificate. Even my driver's license says Siobhán. Sometimes I forget it altogether."

"Unless you need it for kosher food."

"Right."

"Btw. How was the schnitzel?"

"It was delish."

"So Israel?"

"I'm going to work on a kibbutz. Do a little sightseeing."

"So no conversion?" I asked with a smile.

"Nope. I am Irish Catholic through and through. I sang in our church choir."

"Shprintza though, seriously? It is honestly kinda hard to believe. Your father must have been very supportive."

"You need to understand the Irish and our superstitions. Everything is a sign. My pa couldn't compete against a sign."

"I thought it was good luck to be named after a Saint."

And then Shprintza Siobhán Rooney, in her thick southie accent said, "Nah, that is a bubbe meise."

I THOUGHT IT WAS CUTE

My brother once asked me if I valued honesty or whether I preferred he tell me he loved every story I wrote.

I replied quickly and unequivocally: I do not value honesty at all. I am not contemplating quitting my job, mortgaging my house, or putting my family at risk in order to pursue a pipe dream of being a writer. I am a 62-year-old man who has embarked on what can only be generously described as a quasi-vanity project.

With emphasis on vanity. Why would I be interested in the truth?

But it got me thinking about feedback.

My cousin Morris has a passion for music. He writes his own songs and records all the instruments in a make-shift studio in his basement. He is a pretty accomplished guitar player. He puts his heart and soul into creating music and then sends it out to friends and family in order to get feedback. I am sure he would continue to make music even if it were only for himself. But it is human nature to seek validation from our peers. Some of us seek and need it more than others. Morris gets miffed if we take more than 48 hours to get back to him. He will sometimes follow up and ask if we received his email. Truth be told, it is a four-minute song and not such a hard thing to do for my first cousin and good friend. I wish I could say I like all of his songs but that is not always the case. For those songs, I try to find something positive to say. "I really liked the guitar solo in the middle." I never say, "It was not my favorite."

My brother argues that saying things like, "It's not your best," is actually a way of acknowledging he thinks I am a good writer, have written better things in the past, and he expects more from me. He might be right. If he forwards a piece to a friend or colleague at work, I know he found some merit in it.

My editor Jules will say " this one is good for friends and family." That's his way of saying it is not good enough to make the collection.

My friend Carainn will sometimes say, "Ce n'est pas de mon gout." It's not her cup of tea. I guess, in part, comments like this give weight to her more effusive praise.

My friend Steve subscribes to the theory that if you have nothing good to say then say nothing at all. I almost never hear back from him.

The same is true of my friend Arthur- who I golf with in Florida. Once, when we reached the third hole of the golf course, which is the setting of my story Waiting for Zakarian, I said to him 'you should read that story. I think you will like it.' And he said ' I did read it.' So I waited for a compliment. But it didn' come. Instead, he said " It's your shot."

My friend Ellen tells me she loves everything. She supports me unreservedly. I could send her a grocery list and she would love it

Back in the day, when a date didn't call me back, she would say maybe her answering machine was broken.

I tell every waitress dinner was delish. What is to be gained by saying I wouldn't feed it to a Guantanamo prisoner?

I think Morris likes it when I tell him that I loved the guitar solo in the middle.

I don't think he and I are fools. We know the truth. We just prefer to look for our own truths.

I tell my brother I don't value honesty. Find one positive thing to say. It's not so hard.

Some people are good-hearted but turn themselves into a pretzel trying to find the positive. "Such an interesting article." "It was really cute." "I didn't know poker could be so complicated." But I am okay with that.

My friend Snowbird told me he liked the color of the typewriter on the cover. Nice shade of green he said. Larry is an artist so maybe it was a real compliment.

Others are really good at finding something to compliment. My friend Joel Mickelson quoted a line back to me and said it was "brilliant." I genuinely believe Joel liked the piece, but even if he hadn't, his feedback was nothing short of genius and it raised my spirits for the entire week.

Sometimes, "it was really cute" means just that. "It was really cute" is good. I would be happy with that.

My friend Harold Rosen flips things around. He almost always likes all of my stories but still manages to find at least one thing wrong in order to keep me honest. He gets invested in the stories and characters and lets me know if I veer off the path.

My friend Karen, who is both a psychiatrist and an avid poker player, is always very supportive but also quick to point out things which don't make sense in her world. I have a story called Bad Beat where the main character makes a decision out of spite which also penalizes him financially. Karen says no self-respecting poker player would ever do that.

Who ever said anything about self-respect?

The Country Club where I spend the winter has a book club. Every month they send out an email telling us which book they are reading. And every month my friend Paulie, who also has a home here, sends me an email with one line: " they are fucking you again." It is his way of showing his support. My friend Larry did him one better, he emailed the events director in order to try and get me on the list.

I'm still waiting.

My cousin David sent me a text message about the opening act of a Dylan concert we had seen together in 1975. I had no idea what the hell he was talking about. It turns out he was referencing a piece I had written about the opening act for a Santana concert I had seen. He was letting me know he had gone on my website and read a story.

He didn't say it was good.

But that was still nice.

One of the recurring characters in some of my stories is called Lewberg. Lewberg is very very loosely based on a very good friend of mine. Those of you who know him have already guessed. My friend was at lunch with his wife the other day when she turned to him and said, "Can I ask you a question?" He said sure without knowing what to expect. She then said, "Are you Lewberg?"

I love that story.

Life imitating art.

I don't understand people who look for and invariably find typos. It isn't Where's Waldo. Someone asked me why I didn't capitalize an I.

Seriously?

My friend Helen was my first real editor and the person whose opinion I value the most. She is not a fan of my lack of quotation marks and shoddy punctuation. I tell her it is my writing style. She calmly tells me bad grammar is not a style.

I often tell people the only two acceptable responses are "I really liked it" or "I loved it." Sometimes they will reply that they really did love it, despite me saying that was the only acceptable response.

That was nice.

I like hearing nice things. Often, more than often, it makes my day.

I don't think I would write if I couldn't share. Maybe. But I don't think so.

While I think I am more needy and insecure than most, I don't think it is odd to want to hear nice things.

Like the rat in the lab, I go back to the piece of cheese which gave me a pleasurable jolt.

It reminds me to try to say nice things too. I am not always successful, but I am trying.

It costs nothing.

A short story is not a four-minute song. It requires time and concentration. It goes without saying I understand and realize it is an indulgence to ask this from my friends and family.

I really appreciate it.

I would like to think I would do the same but suspect I might ask if I could just write a cheque instead.

So thank you.

And if you need to, go ahead and tell me you really loved the paragraph in the middle.

I'm okay with it.

ABOUT THE AUTHOR

Aaron Zevy is a writer and publisher from Toronto, Canada. He is the author of *Almost the Truth: Stories and Lies*. His children's books, *No Nuts for Me*, *Once Upon a Breath*, *A Light in the Darkness*, and *Bad For Them Good for Me* have been read by hundreds of thousands of kids, parents, and teachers in over 100 countries around the world.

The Bubbe Meise and Other Stories is his second story collection.

Made in the USA
Middletown, DE
19 August 2024

59459563R00130